HOW
TO KNOW
GOD
EXISTS

SOLID REASONS TO BELIEVE IN GOD, DISCOVER TRUTH, AND FIND MEANING IN YOUR LIFE

JOSH D. McDOWELL
THOMAS WILLIAMS

TYNDALE
MOMENTUM®

A Tyndale nonfiction imprint

Visit Tyndale online at tyndale.com.

Visit Tyndale Momentum online at tyndalemomentum.com.

Tyndale, Tyndale's quill logo, *Tyndale Momentum*, and the Tyndale Momentum logo are registered trademarks of Tyndale House Ministries. Tyndale Momentum is a nonfiction imprint of Tyndale House Publishers, Carol Stream, Illinois.

How to Know God Exists: Solid Reasons to Believe in God, Discover Truth, and Find Meaning in Your Life

An earlier edition of this book was previously published in 2003 as *In Search of Certainty* by Tyndale House Publishers under ISBN 978-0-8423-7972-4.

Designed by Jennifer Phelps

Edited by Donna L. Berg

For information about special discounts for bulk purchases, please contact Tyndale House Publishers at csresponse@tyndale.com, or call 1-855-277-9400.

Library of Congress Cataloging-in-Publication Data

A catalog record for this book is available from the Library of Congress.

ISBN 978-1-4964-6122-3

Printed in the United States of America

28	27	26	25	24	23	22
7	6	5	4	3	2	1

CONTENTS

QUESTIONS EVERYONE WANTS ANSWERED

Where did I come from? What is the meaning of life? How can I know right from wrong? What will happen to me after I die? Does God exist? These questions are embedded within each one of us. Trending generational differences may have shifted the emphasis, and the growing dominance of a secular outlook has attempted to override them. Yet these primal concerns are still shared by everyone on the planet.

In the past few decades it has been fashionable to categorize how Americans think by analyzing the beliefs and attitudes of the generations in which they were born. As with any such categorization, there are differing opinions about how to sort the generations, and there will always be exceptions and overlap between groupings. Still, a brief overview can provide a point of reference for understanding how our values and beliefs have changed over time.

Let's start with the Silent Generation, born during the

Great Depression and World War II. Members of this group are typically conservative, religious, and financially secure. Next are the Baby Boomers, born after the war, many of whom rebelled against social norms and instigated the countercultural protests of the 1960s. Members of Generation X, born between 1965 and 1980, tend to be resistant to government and have liberal views on social issues. Millennials, born in 1981 and later, are usually better educated and more tech-savvy than earlier generations but less likely to endorse the norms of religion, race, sexuality, and politics of their predecessors. Members of Generation Z, which began with the year 1997, are commonly considered more independent, less social but more socially conscious, more inward-turned, and more technologically dependent.

We don't doubt that these characterizations of the general mindsets of the generations carry considerable weight. We can see the changes in the approach to life, beliefs, morals, and culture as we study the values adopted by each succeeding generation—changes affecting economics, communication, health, entertainment, government, education, and religion. The trend has been away from traditional values, religious belief, and social responsibility. It has moved toward hedonism, materialism, secularism, and self-sufficiency.

Yet those troublesome questions about origins, meaning, morality, eternity, and God's existence remain.

You may be holding this book because you have reached a place in your life where these questions have risen up to confront you. You may have begun to feel that the faith you embraced in the past no longer has the answers you need. Perhaps the answers offered by secular culture seem as if they might better fit the realities you encounter. If this describes you—or if you are concerned about someone who is facing these questions—we urge you to accompany us on a journey to discover the answers. This is no mere excursion into trivialities dressed in platitudes written in typical religious-book jargon. We will lead you to solid answers that we will demonstrate to be firmly rooted in reality. We will show you that truth is a firm reality you can know with certainty and that meaning is possible when you align yourself with that truth.

We will begin our journey in chapter one by exploring the misconceptions inherent in secularism that have blocked off the light of truth from modern culture. Then in part one of the book, we will consider how to find and rely on the bedrock truths that have underscored successful and satisfying lives throughout the past twenty centuries. We will show that God is no fantasy and demonstrate undeniable steps of reason that can lead you to certainty that he is real.

In part two we will examine the weaknesses of several secular and naturalistic props to atheism, especially those explaining ultimate origins. We will demonstrate through reason, scientific evidence, and the writings of prominent scientists how secular origin theories often contradict science, reason, and observable reality.

(By the way, when we use the terms *naturalism* or *naturalistic*, we mean the philosophy that asserts that nature is all that exists, that there is no supernatural realm, and that there is no transcendent God who exists outside or above nature. There may be shades of difference between naturalism, materialism, secularism, and atheism, but we will use naturalism as a convenient term to encompass these and similar beliefs that exclude God.)

In part three, we will turn a corner and focus on how belief in God provides the only viable foundation for meaning and embodies the truth that bathes the world in beauty and joy. In the final chapter, we will give you a brief overview of the essential foundations undergirding Christian beliefs and show that Christianity is not a fantasy but a demonstrable reality.

Lest you fear that we are about to bombard you with Bible verses and Scripture proof texts to support our claims, we assure you that we will not. In fact, you may find this to be one of the strangest Christian books you've ever read. Nowhere in these pages do we support our arguments with biblical references. We realize that biblical proofs would be meaningless if you are skeptical of religion. Instead, we make every attempt to rely solely on reason, observation, evidence, and common sense in supporting our propositions and reaching our conclusions.

This book began as an update of a previous work titled *In Search of Certainty*, written by the two of us in 2003. Perceiving a rising need to address the secular mindset that now dominates Western culture, we have added considerable new material and reframed much of the content. Essentially, we ended up with an altogether new book. As we tackle head-on the questions that people of all generations are beginning to ask, we trust that it will help you find stability in a society rapidly descending into chaos. More importantly, we believe that it will reassure you that God does indeed exist.

Josh McDowell
Thomas Williams

AN ODD THING HAPPENED WHEN WE GOT RID OF GOD

*Can we thrive in the disenchanted
world of postmodern secularism?*

It was Melissa's first day back in the office after spending a week in a hospital room with her critically injured husband. On the night of the accident he had slipped into a coma, and the doctors offered no hope that he would survive until morning. After four days on life support, however, he suddenly awakened. His vital signs stabilized, and the astounded doctors announced that he would recover completely.

As Melissa explained the harrowing ordeal at the morning coffee break, a friend asked what the doctors had done to induce her husband's dramatic turnaround. "It wasn't the doctors," she replied. "It was prayer. Our entire church prayed for Robert. It was a miracle that healed my husband."

Melissa's coworkers suddenly seemed completely engrossed in the contents of their coffee cups. One man finally responded, "Well, we're all glad your husband will recover,

Melissa. And you have a right to believe whatever you want. But surely there's a more rational explanation."

"Thanks, Jim," Melissa replied. "I appreciate your kind words. But don't you think it makes sense to believe God answers our prayers?"

"Well, it's just that in this day and age, a God who performs magic tricks on demand seems about as realistic as a genie in a bottle."

"Okay, Jim," said his supervisor. "This is probably not the best place or time for that discussion." Amiable conversation never regained its footing, and before long, everyone found an excuse to return to work.

Why does talking about God seem awkward, intrusive, or even offensive in everyday conversation? This question was posed recently on a Christian website. One woman responded, "It is quite hard to discuss how you feel about God and Jesus because many people now are ignorant of what it means to be a person of faith." She added that her friends often made comments like "Stop talking about random crap that didn't happen."[1] Another respondent wrote, "It's odd, isn't it? You can talk about the weather or work but you say 'God' and everyone runs away from you!"[2]

The underlying reason for today's reticence to engage in God-talk is no mystery. A robust belief in Christianity is so foreign to today's culture that even bringing it up in conversation is like ordering a hamburger at a Weight Watchers luncheon. Common reactions to religious belief go something like this: "How can anyone be so backward as to believe in such a fairy tale?" "How can anyone put blind faith above solid reason and scientific evidence?" "In this day and age, no thinking person believes in creation over evolution."

The dominant forces of Western culture no longer endorse belief in the supernatural. The concept of a transcendent realm existing above the natural world is seen as a hollow echo from humanity's immature past, when superstition allowed gods to reign and angels to roam. The dominant voices of modern culture have largely discredited the idea of a supernatural God as a childish fable. Richard Dawkins put modern antipathy to religion in even stronger terms: "[Faith] is capable of driving people to such dangerous folly that faith seems to me to qualify as a kind of mental illness."[3] Secularity now saturates the cultural atmosphere, leaving religion little space to draw the breath of life.

Humanity's Enchanted Past

There was a time when these positions were inverted. Before the advent of modernity, God or gods permeated human history. As Canadian philosopher Charles Taylor puts it, "People lived in an enchanted world, a world 'charged' with presences, that was open and vulnerable, not closed and self-sufficient." He added that in such a world "atheism comes close to being inconceivable."[4]

Taylor explains that in the ancient world, religion was so pervasive that disbelief was almost unthinkable. From their beginning, the ancient Hebrews believed tenaciously in a single omnipotent deity. In the pre-Christian centuries, gods abounded, and belief in their existence was the default mode of almost all known societies. The Greeks and Romans had a god for every known human action and attribute—Mars, the god of war; Venus, the god of love; Pallas Athena, the goddess of wisdom; Apollo, the god of poetry. Athenian Greeks of the first century were so concerned about inadvertently offending deities that they erected a monument "to the unknown god" to be sure they honored all of them. Then, Christianity came along with its concept of one God, sweeping through much of the ancient world and eventually dominating the West. As a result, by late medieval times, belief in a supreme deity was woven so tightly into the fabric of reality that it was almost impossible not to believe. The Christian religion was the ether in which people lived, breathed, and had their being.

Nearly everyone accepted that the natural world was not the sum of reality. Nature was overlaid by a greater, supernatural dimension from which it drew its meaning. The pervasive belief was that nature was created, sustained, and guided by an omnipotent, supernatural being. Invisible, living intelligences attended this being, crossing the boundary between the natural and supernatural realms at will and influencing the affairs of humans for better or worse. As Taylor put it—using an engaging term which we will borrow throughout this chapter—the natural world was "enchanted."

Through the whole of humanity's past, belief in this enchantment of nature by supernatural presences of one kind or another was universal, taken for granted, and assumed as the obvious structure of reality. For both the Christian and the pagan, a viable alternative to belief in God or gods could hardly be imagined.

The Rise of Secularism

You are no doubt aware that this is not the world we Westerners live in now. Belief in God is no longer the default position. The enchanted forest has been felled by the axe of secularism. Christianity, long the West's dominant proclaimer of God, is in retreat, fighting a rearguard, defensive battle against a culture dominated by institutions that no longer find God believable or relevant.

How did Christianity lose its grip on the West? It may seem that the change came quickly within the past few decades. In fact, it was a change long in the making and impacted by many complex factors and events. It would be impossible to cover all of the influences thoroughly here, and we acknowledge that others might interpret them a little differently than we do. To provide a groundwork for our discussion, however, it will be beneficial to briefly consider those we feel have been most significant.

As Taylor points out, the shift began some five hundred years ago with the Reformation, a sixteenth-century movement instigated to purify Christianity but instead eroding it with unintended consequences.

Before the Reformation, the Catholic church dominated

European culture. Principled reformers such as Martin Luther, John Calvin, and John Knox, and less principled ones such as England's King Henry VIII, fractured the monolithic church into denominational splinters. Suddenly people were faced with theological choices. No longer subject to a single ecclesiastical authority, they became choosers, masters of their own theological destiny. This new and heady power of individual choice diminished the communal unity that came with shared belief. Like sheep escaping through a broken fence, believers exchanged the security of the flock for a new sense of personal freedom.

The enchantment—the sense of a world infused with supernatural transcendence—was further diminished by the rise of the eighteenth-century Enlightenment philosophers. René Descartes, John Locke, Immanuel Kant, and others promoted reason as the primary tool for determining truth. This move eventually demoted faith to the false position of unfounded belief. Then in the mid-nineteenth century, Charles Darwin's theories of evolution rendered God unnecessary even as Creator, making it possible for humans to live in a world completely free of any need for the supernatural. As Richard Dawkins says, "Darwin made it possible to be an intellectually fulfilled atheist."[5]

In the nineteenth and twentieth centuries, science and industry further dispelled the enchantment. In World War II, America turned out an unprecedented volume of military weapons, planes, and ships and developed atomic energy into a force that effectively ended the war. Brimming with postwar power, the nation's booming factories immediately began producing wealth and economic opportunity for its citizens. Within a few decades, there was a car in almost every garage, a TV in every home, and scores of appliances to do the hard labor that formerly dominated humanity's waking hours. Modern medicine almost doubled human life expectancy. Today science, technology, and industry provide us not only with necessities, conveniences, and health, but also with luxuries and entertainment beyond our ancestors' most fevered imaginations.

These spectacular accomplishments put science on a pedestal, which the dominant scientific establishment used as a pulpit for proclaiming that nature is a closed system. Soon the idea that nothing exists outside the natural world became settled knowledge in secular education. As the late Carl Sagan put it, "The Cosmos is all that is or ever was or ever will be."[6] This belief that nature is all there is became dominant. Most scientists boldly expressed confidence that mysteries that presently seem supernatural will in time be explained as one more cog in the self-originated, self-perpetuating machine that nature is. (We recognize, of course, that there are many scientists of faith, and even some secular scientists, who do not hold to this view.)

The dominant institutions of the West essentially accepted this disenchantment of the supernatural as reality. Education distilled it into curricula and disseminated it as settled knowledge. God became superfluous as man flexed his power to take charge of his own destiny. With the spirits thus banished from the machine that is nature, we now live in a mechanistic world insulated from the supernatural. Thanks to the diligence of science and industry, we have at the flip of a switch, the pressing of a button, the turn of a dial, or the punching of a keyboard everything we need to make life worth living without reference to the God or gods of our ancestors. The enchantment is broken.

Living in the Disenchanted World

With the world thus disenchanted, we see nature differently than did our ancestors. The universe is now nothing more than a machine that burst into existence accidentally and chugs along blindly. With no creator to give it purpose, no meaning can be ascribed to it. It has no goal and no destination. It merely spins along in the circular orbits of atoms, planets, and galaxies. It is going nowhere. Therefore, we can no longer regard components of nature in terms of their ends—the *why* behind their existence. There can be no why in an accidental universe. With God excluded, we now see everything simply in terms of its functional mechanism.

This loss of meaning brought about a significant change not only in the way we see nature, but also in the way we live. Before the disenchantment, most of the Western world found meaning in the Christian God's promise of a transcendent eternity. Living under this promise placed responsibilities on us, and we dared not live as if we belonged solely to ourselves. We held virtue, truth, and morality to be God-ordained and believed our lives should be ordered accordingly. Despite our many and spectacular failures to live up to this ideal, we believed that God's love remained intact and his plan of redemption atoned for our guilt. When modernity did away with the concept of a supernatural god, it extinguished this Christian expectation of eternity, leaving us to find meaning solely within the mechanized system of nature and within the human birth-to-death life span.

It might seem that we humans would find this change traumatizing. We are now isolated, alone, exposed, and unprotected in a cold universe that spawned us blindly and cares nothing for our destiny—a universe going nowhere and leaving us with nowhere to go. Gone is the comfort of knowing our lives are cradled in the arms of a loving creator who offers a glorious, eternal future. Humanity is now merely a collection of disparate individuals with no shared system of belief and no path to significance, living in an accidental universe without purpose or meaning. The sense of loss should be overwhelming.

A sense of loss did occur, but it was offset by a grand sense of accomplishment. In abolishing the transcendent supernatural realm, humans felt that they had done a courageous thing. It freed us to choose our own path, unshackled by the constraints of deity. The banishment of God freed us from the burden of virtue, the restrictions of morality, and the weight of truth. We no longer had limits on how we fulfilled our desires. We were now free to find meaning on our own terms and rebuild the world in our own image, according to our own liking. This is why prominent atheists like George

Bernard Shaw could purportedly quip, "I'm an atheist and I thank God for it."[7]

To clear the ground for this new tower of humanism, modernity morphed into postmodernity. Modernism as a philosophy tended away from belief in the supernatural and based its concept of truth on reason applied to the findings of science and Enlightenment philosophy. Postmodernism eroded modernism by doubting the validity of any truth claim and asserting that our reasoning capacity is too limited and our defining narratives too subjective to be dependable. With the advent of postmodernity, all authority and all restrictions on our beliefs and actions were questioned. Absolute truth claims were now seen as intolerant. Man would henceforth determine truth for himself. Moral law lost its authority and became an intrusion on our right to pursue any pleasure. Virtually all human desires became normalized, and sexual freedom became the rallying banner of the new order. Moral restrictions on literature, movies, TV, and the Internet were loosened or lifted. Cohabitation, pornography, homosexuality, gay marriage, and transgenderism shed their centuries-old stigma and flowed into the mainstream. The right to abortion became a crucial underpinning of sexual freedom to protect against consequences formerly prevented by moral behavior.

As the twenty-first century began, this new secular order became thoroughly infused into the West's most influential institutions, including government, education, media, entertainment, sports, and business. These institutions have done much to eradicate God from Western culture and pave the way for us to assert ourselves as the masters of our own fate and captains of our own souls. As a result, any sense that we humans have an ultimate purpose has been largely eclipsed by the idea that this world itself can be ordered for our benefit without waiting for pie in the sky by and by.

The Downside of Disenchantment

While this brave new world exulted in the sunlight of its newfound liberty, deep in the shadows lurked an uneasy emptiness that secularism simply could not fill. Meaning and purpose—so easy to find under a transcendent God—disappeared in the closed-off universe of modernity. It soon became apparent that in the new secular order, meaning simply does not exist. Many now feel this emptiness, which is generating an increase in disillusionment, depression, and suicide. Perhaps you have felt this in your own life or seen it in the lives of those around you.

The rise in depression and suicide has been well documented. According to a Columbia University study, "Depression increased significantly among persons in the U.S. from 2005 to 2015, from 6.6 percent to 7.3 percent. Notably, the rise was most rapid among those ages 12 to 17, increasing from 8.7 percent in 2005 to 12.7 percent in 2015."[8] In 2020 the Centers for Disease Control (CDC) reported that US suicide rates increased by 35 percent from 1999 to 2018.[9] Suicide is currently the twelfth leading cause of death in the US.[10]

To counter the temptation to seek meaning and purpose by reverting to religious belief, the new order has been diligent to reinforce the value of secularism. It does this by promoting stoicism, independence, and consumerism.

Stoicism: Buck Up

For the philosophically turned, secularism offers a sort of stoicism. Yes, we are told, the secular universe may lack meaning and purpose. It's true that our lives have no significance and are headed nowhere, but it's better to face and accept this hard reality than to seek false comfort in the fantasy that religion offers. As British philosopher Julian Baggini put it, "The reason to be an atheist is not that it makes us feel better or gives us a more rewarding life. The reason to be an atheist is simply that there is no God and we would prefer to live in full recognition of that, accepting the consequences, even if it makes us less happy."[11]

We admire such stoic dedication to a less-than-comforting belief. To maintain that dedication, secularists must exert ongoing effort. They must continually remind themselves of their belief that modernity has discredited religion and that the natural universe is all there is. Therefore, purpose and meaning do not exist. They are illusions fobbed off on us by religion. Secularists must never stop reminding themselves that atheism is reality. Face up to it. Repeat it over and over. We must now be strong enough to live in a world without meaning—a world going nowhere.

Independence: Be Yourself

Secularism also reinforces the disenchantment by offering independence as an alternative to purpose and meaning. Assert your individuality. Be yourself. Create the person you want to be by exercising your freedom from the restrictive boundaries of religion. Since values no longer exist, choice is valued above what is chosen. It's not important that you choose the right thing (is there such a thing as right?) or that you choose the truth (is there such a thing as truth?). But it is crucial that you choose something in order to define yourself and give yourself a sense of control. "I choose, therefore I am." Choose your own politics, your own causes, your own morality, your own truth, your own sexual orientation, even your own sex. Choice attempts to validate the independent self by making each person his or her own agent in constructing a life without conforming to an ideal imposed from above.

We soon find, however, that individual autonomy is not sufficient to supply meaning. We seem to have not only a built-in need for independence, but also a corresponding need for community. The old fabric of a transcendent shared belief that formerly wove us together has been ripped away, and replacements are hard to come by.

This double-sided need for both autonomy and community has opened an enormous marketing opportunity for corporations and advertisers. To meet that need (and fatten their bank accounts), they induce us to autonomously choose conformity. Advertising has succeeded in making us think we're asserting our independence when we choose to be like virtually everyone else. We are manipulated into accepting the illusion of individuality as we subconsciously choose the conformity of fashion—not merely the fashion of clothing, foods, cars, or hairstyles, but also whatever beliefs or causes are currently in vogue. Notice how popular causes come and go—causes that everyone with a social conscience must adhere to while they are popular. Next year the causes pursued so avidly today will lose their luster, and individuals seeking autonomy will flock en masse to new ones. Fashion counterfeits community by luring us into a fabricated conformity. The common ground of fashion enables us to make "self-expressive" choices that gain us acceptance by duplicating the choices of the group whose approval we value. Be yourself! Break from the herd and flaunt your individuality by purchasing this product that everyone else is buying.

Consumerism: Eat, Drink, and Be Merry

The masking of lockstep conformity under the guise of independent choice leads to the most common attempt to banish enchantment from the lives of moderns—consumerism. Consumerism feeds on an accelerated cycle of pop-up desires and transient fulfillments. It provides extended distraction from the emptiness left by the loss of transcendence. Eat, drink, and be merry. Fill your existence with sensation to obliterate the awareness of that gnawing hole in your life.

Awareness of this lack of meaning began to emerge during the youth rebellions of the 1960s. In 1969 the legendary Peggy Lee recorded her hit song, "Is That All There Is?" Each verse expresses extreme disillusionment with events in which she expected to find deep significance. As a child, she watches her house burn down; her father takes her to a circus; she grows up and falls in love. But none of these events gives her the depth of meaning she expected. So, after describing each, she sings the dreary repeating chorus, "Is that all there is? If that's all there is my friends, then let's keep dancing. Let's break out the booze and have a ball—if that's all there is."[12]

In a disenchanted world, the best we can do is drown the craving for meaning in a sea of sensation. Calvin University philosophy professor James K. A. Smith states it more specifically: "Most of the time the best 'salvation' we can hope for is found in behaviors that numb us to this reality: drugs, sex, entertainments of various sorts."[13] These behaviors, however, are like packing with Bubble Wrap the space meant to hold a treasure. Everything we cram into the void turns out to be as empty as the void itself. With the loss of transcendence, we still lack meaning and direction. We are empty vessels heading nowhere.

The Dogged Persistence of Transcendence

Most secularists soon become aware that with the banishment of transcendence they have lost any hope of finding a valid concept of meaning and purpose. As we have noted, their response to that loss may be admirable and courageous—face up to it and move on. They think that humanity's freedom from the shackles of religion and independence in a world without God should be enough to bury the desire for meaning and purpose.

The problem, as so many have found, is that this desire will not stay buried. Banishing God from reality may be a momentous accomplishment, but it has left us with a gaping emptiness. As novelist Julian Barnes quipped, "I don't believe in God, but I miss him."[14]

Charles Taylor has noted that this emptiness often is felt most deeply in events we recognize as the most significant passages in life—birth, marriage, and death. The depth of meaning we expect to find in these milestones often is missing, leaving us with an emotional flatness. Like Peggy Lee, we ask, "Is that all there is?" Committed secularists may search for a way to ascribe meaning to such events, but their immersion in the disenchanted world of postmodernity precludes it. It allows them to see only the machine that is nature chugging blindly through its meaningless cycle, robotically churning out new life while endlessly discarding the old.

Yet death inevitably brings thoughts of eternity to even the most secular heart. The passing of a dear friend or family member throws secularists into a state of circular confusion with a persistent sense that the life that just ended could not just end. They may be convinced intellectually that the existence of their loved one has ceased forever, but something within resists such a fatalistic conclusion. The conviction that she is obliterated forever pushes hard against the impossibility of thinking of her as no longer existing. And a sense that her existence had meaning pushes hard against the postmodern denial of meaning.

It's not uncommon for death to be a serious problem for atheists. One woman, seeking advice for dealing with death, wrote to an atheist website, saying,

> I am afraid of dying. I am so afraid of dying that if I think about what it would mean, even for a second, I become fixated on the thought and have a panic attack where I reach the point of almost passing out. It only happens every once in a while, and I am a fully functioning person, but if I do think about it I can't function. . . . Deep down I wish I could believe in a god, just to make the fear go away. . . . I thought about therapy, but therapy would mean confronting it and I don't think I could, because what's the end result? Either I fool myself into thinking that there is paradise or another life waiting for me or I keep this knowledge hidden from myself, always waiting to reemerge as I've been trying to do all of my life.[15]

Facing such fears, we long for more than secularism can deliver. This woman can neither face down death nor ignore the question it raises about the afterlife she no longer believes in. Peter Steele, the late lead singer of the goth-metal band Type O Negative, put it this way: "When you start to think about death, you start to think about what's after it. And then you start hoping there is a God."[16]

At such moments a yearning for eternity surfaces, and this yearning gives evidence that the desire for transcendence is neither childish nor superficial, as secularism proclaims it to be. We must either accept it as a realistic possibility or dismiss it as an illusion that has persistently haunted humanity from its beginning and refuses to be exorcised.

Secularism can bury the human longing for transcendence, but it cannot kill it. Nor can we dig a grave deep enough to prevent its reemergence. Eventually, it will claw its way out and present itself as a serious challenge to secular disenchantment. The self cannot endure the closed-off system of modernity indefinitely. Eventually, dissatisfaction with life shut out from meaning and purpose becomes unbearable.

The Secular Clash with Christianity

Christianity has always offered a clear and rational path to meaning and purpose. But the problem is that the principles of Christianity are radically out of sync with the new secular order. This means its attractions must be discredited and its influence curbed if secularism is to flourish. To prevent defections of disillusioned souls seeking meaning and purpose, secularists know they must root Christianity out of the dominant institutions of society and either silence it or confine it to the margins.

This explains why opposition to Christianity has become

increasingly intense in the past few decades. It explains why prayer, the Bible, Christmas, the Ten Commandments, and positive references to Christianity have been excluded from public schools, universities, government, courthouses, entertainment, and even many businesses. High schools and universities prohibit valedictorians from mentioning their faith. Many campuses bar Christian organizations from meeting in their facilities. Christian employees who express or act on their beliefs in schools or workplaces often face disciplinary action, fines, job termination, or lawsuits. Businesses have been boycotted, sued, and even forced to close when their beliefs no longer align with the changing standards of secular moralism.

When you look at Christianity from the secularist's point of view, it's easy to see why it is so vociferously opposed. Christianity is denounced as false because most scientists have proclaimed that the supernatural does not exist. It is denounced as irrational because it is accused of basing its beliefs on blind faith. It is denounced as evil because it is perceived as subjugating women, ignoring social justice, opposing sexual freedom, and discriminating against gays and transgendered persons. It is denounced as intolerant because it does not endorse the authenticity of other religions. It is denounced as politically incorrect because it insists that truth is real and absolute, which clashes with today's postmodern climate of fluid truth and self-determined morality.

Secularists oppose Christianity because it runs counter to the foundational principles they accept as real or as desirable goals—the sexual revolution, self-autonomy, deep trust in the pronouncements of scientists, the fluidity of truth and morality. Secularism is the intellectual, political, and religious air we now breathe. To keep the cultural atmosphere pure, Christianity must be treated as a pollutant.

Breaking from the Lockstep

Today the dominant institutions of Western society actively promote the negative assessment of Christianity outlined above. Moreover, they are increasingly successful in bringing the populace around to their view.

It is true that Christianity holds to many principles that secularism does not endorse, and it rejects many principles that secularism does endorse. We assure you, however, that *authentic* Christianity is nothing like the distorted parody that secularism presents. As happens with any religion, political organization, or cultural conviction, some who claim to be committed proponents of their cause actually represent it very poorly. Christians who behave badly naturally lead people to accept as valid the current condemnation of Christianity. But Christianity's core beliefs contain none of the bigotry, intolerance, or judgmentalism it is accused of. If the misinformation thrust at you by entertainment, media, and education has led you to consider writing off Christianity, we can't blame you. If their claims reflected the truth about Christianity, we would reject it ourselves. We can understand why many today simply accept what the dominant secular institutions feed them and feel no need to dig deeper. Without accurate information to guide them, they naturally join the rush to condemn what they see as an obstinate, backward-looking religion that refuses to board the progressive train. At some point, however, many on that train begin to realize it is progressing toward no definitive destination. It's going nowhere.

If you are a person of faith, perhaps you have been toying with the idea of abandoning your past belief system and boarding the progressive train. If so, in the following pages we will reassure you that God is real and give you solid reasons for continuing to trust in him. Or, maybe you have never endorsed a Christian belief system but find an emptiness in your life that causes you to wonder about secularism's claims. In the following pages, we will show you that the God of Christianity does exist and walk you through the sound reasons for believing in this monolithic truth. We understand that you may feel a strong resistance to what you have been culturally conditioned to reject. One of the most difficult tasks any of us can undertake is an honest reexamination of our own foundational beliefs. Yet if humanity's persistent craving for purpose and meaning has begun to eat at you, and if you have come to realize that secularism offers no valid fulfillment, what do you have to lose by exploring the foundations for belief in God?

Contrary to what our culture contends, the God of Christianity does not demand blind faith. Belief in his existence is rationally defensible. It stands or falls on the basis of logical consistency and rational validation. Our claims that God exists, truth is real, and meaning is embedded in reality are testable. We challenge you to test them for yourself—to step back from the progressive train platform at least long enough to reconsider the possibility that supernatural transcendence may be a reality. Christianity offers a path that will guide you back from the nowhere of secularism to reality itself. It's a journey that will open vistas of meaning and purpose and reveal the hope-filled destiny awaiting you.

In the pages that follow we will present and explain the evidence for a thoroughly rational belief in a transcendent God. We will show how his existence validates our search for meaning. We will show that faith in God is neither an irrational leap into the dark nor a desperate hope without substance. Rather, it is utterly rational, soundly grounded, intellectually defensible, and emotionally fulfilling. We will show that the God of creation is the only complete and rational answer to humanity's religious and philosophic questions, and only by aligning with his truth can we make sense of the reality we experience. You don't have to check your brain at the door of the church to become a believer; you don't have to turn your back on life's joys. In fact, it is our passionate conviction that belief in God is the only cure for society's current malaise and the only source of real contentment and joy.

Just in case you are one of those readers who skips over a book's foreword, we will repeat an assurance we offered there.

If you fear that we are about to bombard you with Bible verses to support our claims, we assure you that we will not. In fact, nowhere in these pages do we support our arguments with biblical references, realizing they would be meaningless to you if you are skeptical of religion. Instead, we make every attempt to rely solely on reason, observation, evidence, and common sense in supporting our propositions.

Our ultimate hope is that this book will help you to see the glimmers of transcendence that break through the barrier of postmodern secularism. We will identify the source of these glimmers, attempt to reassure you that they are real, and—we hope—open your mind to accept the truth of an enchanted universe bathed in meaning, beauty, love, and joy.

QUESTIONS FOR THOUGHT AND DISCUSSION

1. Why does talk about God and Christianity tend to breed hostility in today's culture?

2. Why was disbelief in God or gods of some kind so rare in past ages?

3. How did industrial and scientific advances of the mid-twentieth century foster secularism?

4. Why did getting rid of God rob humankind of a sense of meaning and purpose?

5. What are some of the ways people try to deal with the loss of meaning and purpose? Have you ever felt this loss? How do you account for it? In what ways do you compensate for it?

6. Why has the rise of secularism fostered a rise in depression, anxiety, and suicide?

7. How do watershed events such as marriage, birth, and death shake our confidence in secularism?

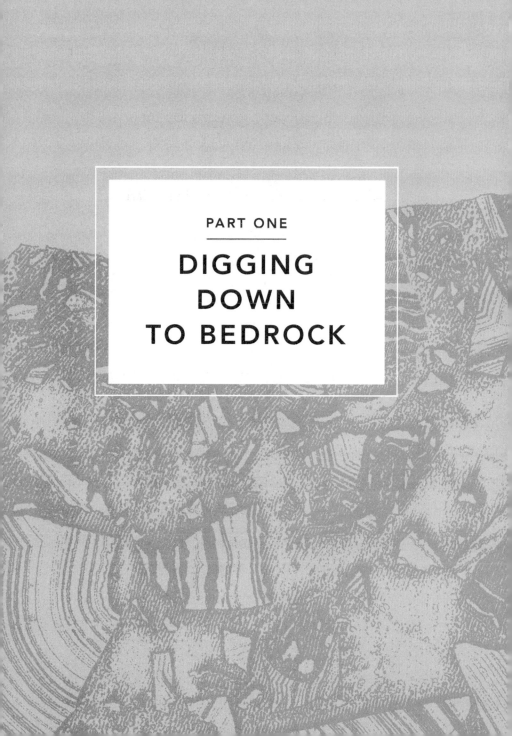

PART ONE

DIGGING
DOWN
TO BEDROCK

2

THE NEED FOR ROCK-SOLID STANDARDS

What do we mean by truth, *and why does it matter?*

It was Saturday morning, and Alex was deep in sleep when his cell phone rang. He groped for it, punched it on, and mumbled, "Hello."

"Hey, Alex," said his longtime friend Kevin. "Are you busy this morning? I need to borrow your pickup—and you too if you're available."

"What's going on?" Alex asked, keeping his voice down to avoid waking his wife.

"I just saw that Walmart has their sixty-five-inch HDR Smart TVs half price, while quantities last. So I need to get there quick. Obviously, I can't take it home on my motorcycle, so I need your truck. Plus, I could use your help loading it."

"Sure, I can do that," said Alex. "I'll leave a note for Sara and pick you up at your apartment."

"No, don't go to my place. I'm at Megan's." He gave Alex the address and hung up.

When Alex arrived, Kevin stood outside the apartment waiting. The moment he got into the pickup, Alex lit into him. "So, did you spend the night with that girl? You know that's not right, Kevin. We've talked about it a thousand times. How can you just thumb your nose at moral standards the way you do?"

"I keep telling you, I've outgrown those churchy rules we grew up with," Kevin replied. "No one who really thinks believes that God stuff anymore. It's just a bunch of superstitions from the Dark Ages, and science has disproved all of it. Those thou-shalt-nots are nothing but a buzzkill."

"God meant for those 'churchy rules' and 'thou-shalt-nots' to help you have a good life," said Alex.

"I don't need a bunch of made-up rules to be happy," Kevin responded. "All those so-called moral standards don't really mean much of anything anymore. We all have to decide what's right for ourselves. I live by my own rules." The argument continued until they reached Walmart.

Kevin found the TV he wanted, but he thought the screen looked smaller than advertised. He consulted a salesclerk, who assured him that the model on display was indeed the correct one. But Kevin still doubted. "Do you have a tape measure?" he asked.

The clerk found a steel tape and helped Kevin measure the screen while Alex watched. The tape confirmed the clerk's claim: the TV measured a full sixty-five inches.

"I guess you're right," admitted Kevin. "It just didn't look that big to me. I'll take it." He checked out with his credit card, and Alex helped him load the TV into the pickup bed.

As they got into the truck, Alex grinned at his friend and said, "I thought you didn't believe in standards for right and wrong."

"I don't," Kevin insisted.

"Then why did you ask for a tape to check the size of the TV?"

"I wanted to get what I paid for."

"And you needed a standard—the tape measure—to be sure Walmart gave you what they advertised. So you do believe we need standards to make sure people do the right thing."

"Oh, come on, Alex. That's different, and you know it."

"Are you sure? You just showed that we need firm standards for measurements. Isn't it possible we need firm standards for behavior, too?"

Kevin agreed with Alex up to a point. He acknowledged the need for a few basic standards to ensure fairness and justice and to keep people honest. But he scoffed at the idea that universal moral standards might exist as objective realities that are always true for all people, at all times, and in all places.

Kevin believes—as today's culture in general believes—that there are no objective standards for morality, and therefore there is no such thing as moral truth. In fact, he believes truth to be a fluid concept that we each determine for ourselves. This means what is true for one may not be true for another. When Kevin uses the word *truth*, he means the guiding principle he personally has chosen to follow. His guiding truth is that his actions should please himself and not hurt anyone else. He believes, therefore, that sex between mutually consenting partners is just as right for him as sex confined to marriage is for Alex. Though Kevin has never bothered to define his guiding philosophy, his "truth" essentially is agnostic materialism, which is rooted in the idea that there is no authority higher than the self.

Here we have set before us two diametrically opposed claims that are presently ripping apart the fabric of Western society: the claim that truth is fluid, adaptable, and self-determined, as opposed to the claim that truth is an absolute reality rooted in a transcendent God. Despite the postmodern devaluation of reason, the rational principle that opposite claims cannot both be true remains intact. This means Alex's claim that absolute truth exists cannot be reconciled with Kevin's claim that absolute truth does not exist. How can we determine which claim reflects reality—if either?

To lay the groundwork for answering that question, we first will explore the use of standards in general—their purpose, their necessity, and especially how they derive their authority.

Sources of Our Common Standards

The origin of standard linear measurements is lost in history. It is assumed that in the past, carpenters sized their lumber by the handiest measuring device available, which was their own foot. As a result, six-foot tables varied in length because carpenters' feet varied in length. It was wise to check out the carpenter's shoe size before placing an order.

As legend has it, a king eventually decided to end the chaotic variations in linear measurements. Some credit England's Henry I; some think it may have been Edward I or II. This king, whoever he was, published the length of his own royal foot and decreed that in his kingdom, this would be the standard for a one-foot measurement. From that point on, anyone who ordered a six-foot table knew precisely what he was getting: a table exactly six times the length of the king's foot.

Conditional, Invented Standards

Just as the king provided a standard for linear measurements in his kingdom, governments today provide standards for the weights and measures we use in everyday commerce. In the United States, these are overseen by the National Institute of Standards and Technology. This government agency maintains fixed standards for the specific length of miles, yards, feet, and inches; the specific volume of gallons, quarts, and pints; and the specific weight of tons, pounds, and ounces.

We depend on these standards daily in practical ways. When we purchase a pound of beef, two yards of fabric, or a quart of milk, we know exactly how much product we will take home. Or when we plan to drive from Dallas to

Nashville at a given rate of speed, we can determine how long the trip will take.

These standards set by governments serve us well by preventing confusion in economics and scheduling. But they are not absolute; they are arbitrarily determined. Let's call them *conditional* standards. They are conditional on the authority that sets them. They can change when the authority behind them changes. A new king may come to power and decide that his size-thirteen foot makes a better standard than his predecessor's size twelve. European governments have changed the standards for weights, volumes, and lengths to the metric system and the medium of exchange from the currency of individual countries to the common euro. Yet despite such changes, we accept these conditional standards and the authority behind them because we know we need commonly accepted standards to stabilize the workings of society.

Unconditional Standards from Nature

Not all our everyday standards are conditional. The standards for measuring time, for example, are unconditional because they are beyond human control. Nature rather than human decision dictates our basic time measurements. A day consists of one cycle of daylight and darkness, which is determined by the rotation of the earth. A year consists of 365.2422 days because that is how long it takes the earth to orbit the sun. Somewhere back in history, some human authority divided the day into twenty-four segments called hours (the ancient Egyptians are often credited), but these segments had to conform to a reality over which humans have no authority—the rotation of the earth. Hours and minutes are conditional, human-contrived standards, but they conform to an unconditional standard that is not subject to human manipulation.

What about Moral Standards?

Kevin, our TV purchaser, believes the standards for truth and morality are like those for lengths, volumes, and weights—they are humanly determined and enforced by human laws and societal consensus. Alex, on the other hand, believes the standards for morality are like those for time. They are based on realities that exist above and beyond human manipulation. Which view is correct? How can we know?

Let's Take a Vote

A story is told of a first-grade child who brought a puppy to school for show-and-tell. In the discussion that followed, the children began to wonder about the sex of the dog, but they were uncertain about how to determine it. A little girl raised her hand and said, "I know how we can tell." The teacher, resigning herself to a discussion of the birds and the bees, said, "Okay, Megan, how can we tell?" The girl replied, "We can vote."

In the recent past, Megan's reply would have induced a chuckle as a cute joke. But today her suggestion for determining reality illustrates the operating assumption that dominates postmodern culture. Whatever people vote for, choose, endorse, or allow carries the weight of truth. Practices widely condemned a few short generations ago—abortion, homosexuality, gender fluidity, euthanasia, pornography, and sexual freedom—are widely accepted today. They are considered right if the governing authority or society or individuals deem them right. Absolute standards for truth and morality are now considered nonexistent, which means we believe ourselves free to decide on our own what is true and what is moral.

If the standards for truth and morality are nothing more than conditional standards imposed on society by civil governments, societal consensus, or church councils, then the secular assessment of morality would be correct. Moral standards would be arbitrary, with no more validity than human authority gives them. If, on the other hand, the standards for truth and morality are more like the standard for time, then they are not arbitrary. They are based on a reality beyond the reach of human influence. Ignoring them would be perilous, for we would be butting our heads against unyielding reality.

To illustrate the point, suppose the government decides that society would be more productive if our days were extended by one hour. To ensure conformity, Congress passes a law changing the length of a day from twenty-four to twenty-five hours. We can imagine the resulting turmoil. The length of a day would no longer conform to the natural cycle of daylight and darkness. It would be out of sync with the twenty-four-hour cycle of the earth's rotation. Sunrise and sunset would occur at a different time each day. Sleep patterns and work hours would become erratic, confusing, and impossible to maintain.

Fighting Gravity

Christianity claims that the standard for truth is like the standard for time. It is absolute and beyond human manipulation; it cannot be changed or modified by human will. When we fail to conform to this externally imposed standard, it is similar to recalibrating the length of a day. Manipulating the standard puts us out of alignment with reality—with the way the universe is set up to run. The chaos caused by misalignment with truth may not be as immediately apparent as messing with the length of a day, but eventually the results will be just as destabilizing. If a rigid, unconditional standard for truth exists, humans will find it impossible to build stable lives on any other foundation, no matter how intensely desired or sincerely believed.

On April 24, 2017, Lucie Bahetoukilae boarded a United Airlines plane in Newark, New Jersey, intending to fly to her home in Paris, France. But she ended up in San Francisco, California. Her ticket contained all the correct information—her flight number, gate number, and the departure point and destination: "Newark to Charles de Gaulle." Because Lucie speaks only French, however, she did not understand that there had been a gate change for her flight. She went to the wrong gate, and the attendant who scanned her ticket failed to catch her mistake.[1]

Throughout the trip, Lucie sincerely believed that she was flying to Paris. But sincerity was not enough to override the truth that when she deboarded that plane, she was in San Francisco. Sincerity about one's mistaken belief, or a strong desire for a belief to be true, will not obligate it to conform to reality.

When we set out to determine our own truth, our choice may be based on preferences, feelings, desires, peer approval, or—as in the case of Lucie Bahetoukilae—mistaken data. Without thorough and accurate information up front, we have no way of knowing the long-term results of our choice. Before the health risks of smoking were known, many took up the habit because it provided pleasurable sensations or seemed to add an aura of sophistication to one's persona. But these "truths" about the benefits of smoking were shattered by lung cancer and heart disease. Arbitrarily chosen beliefs not grounded in reality can lead to unhappy results.

This vast, complex universe we were born into was an established reality long before we came along. Its laws and movements are set in stone and have been operative from the beginning of time. We cannot bend these realities to align with our own proclivities. The universe is not waiting for us to decide what reality should be in order to adapt itself to our desires. It is we who must adapt to the preexisting standards within the universe. We know that attempting to impose our own "truth" upon gravity would be insane. When we stub our toe, we don't expect gravity to give us a pass and refrain from pulling us down to the sidewalk just because the trip was accidental. We get along in the world by learning its realities and adapting our actions accordingly.

Could the same principle apply to morality? To our search for meaning and purpose?

Connecting to a Higher Reality

As we noted in chapter 1, when our secularized world banished God, it also banished all possibility of finding true meaning and purpose. Yet people still long for the significance that meaning and purpose bring. This longing is hard to dismiss as a mere illusion. The very fact that it haunts us strongly suggests that the human psyche is connected—or is meant to be connected—with some external and higher reality. We learn by experience that a meaningful sense of purpose cannot be self-determined. We may find a fleeting sense of meaning and purpose in our careers or our families until we realize that without some connection to transcendence even these highly valued accomplishments and relationships are merely straws in the wind. They are too temporary to provide meaning. In the secular universe, nothing we do or love will last long beyond our lifetimes. If our existence is to have meaning, there must be some transcendent reality outside ourselves to provide it. If we are to have purpose, there must be some external reason for our existence. Because these questions point inevitably to external realities, we cannot answer them by drawing on our own internal resources. They strongly imply that a truth exists outside of and above any "truth" we choose for ourselves. To find meaning and purpose, we must align ourselves with that external, pre-existing truth.

We also noted in the first chapter that secularism tries to dismiss the longing for meaning and purpose as an illusion. Believers in God are convinced otherwise. The very fact that we have a persistent sense of meaning and purpose strongly suggests their reality. If these qualities are mere illusions, there is no natural or rational explanation for why they are embedded in the human psyche. Evolution, conceived and sold to us as a natural process to explain species survival and development, is inadequate to account for the existence of anything in the human mind as unnatural as an illusion. Believers are further convinced that this sense of meaning and purpose is grounded solidly in an ultimate truth upon which the entire universe rests. Hang on while we lead you on a quick journey to identify that truth.

The Search for Ultimate Truth

Our claim that objective truth exists is empty unless we show it to be rooted in an ultimate absolute that ensures its authenticity. There must exist a final authority beyond question to serve as the ultimate answer to all questions. Our claim to knowledge of any kind collapses like a line of falling dominoes unless buttressed by something that can't be knocked over. Before we can determine whether any belief is objectively true, we must find it backed up by something so obviously true that it needs no proof of its own.

The process of finding that truth is much like that of a businessman examining a building before he buys it. He trusts the integrity of the building only when he's assured it rests on a solid foundation. He trusts the integrity of the foundation only when he's assured it is built on bedrock. He trusts bedrock simply because it is bedrock. Experience, reason, and intuition combine to tell us that bedrock is the ultimate answer to solidity. Everyone trusts bedrock without feeling a need to prove its soundness. No one questions it or insists on looking beneath it for something more solid. It is the builder's absolute.

We can determine the validity of our beliefs by following a similar process. To demonstrate, let's take a belief that virtually all people—Christians, agnostics, moderns, secularists, and even postmodernists—accept as right and true: *We should always stop and help a wounded motorist stranded on a lonely highway.* Since this conviction that we should help others in need is virtually universal, is it possible that it is a real, foundational truth—an unconditional standard—that exists independent of human contrivance? Before making that assumption, we should look beneath it to see if it has a supporting foundation.

Our first hint that this principle might not be a humanly contrived conditional standard is that it asks us to act in opposition to our own inclinations, contrary to our own convenience, and sometimes even at the risk of our own safety. Why should I care anything about the well-being of strangers? My primary interest is my own well-being. The mandate to put the needs of another above the wants of self is not natural, which gives us our first hint that it may have come from somewhere outside nature. Can we find a foundation principle that supports this persistent but troublesome belief that I should interrupt my life to help someone else?

When we look for a solid foundation for this belief, we find that it rests on a strong conviction we all carry within us—the conviction that *society ought to be preserved*—that we all have an obligation to promote the continuation of human life on the planet. Virtually all of us, whether we believe in God or not, accept this principle as a foundational truth. It is a universally assumed principle that has been adhered to throughout all history by all societies in all places and in all times.

Though we have found a seemingly solid foundation for our belief that we should help others, we still have not reached bedrock. When we say we should do it because it fosters the preservation of society, we must then ask: Why should society be preserved? Where did that idea come from? Why should it matter to me? Why does almost everyone think of the preservation of ongoing human life as a foundational tenet to which all humans should dedicate themselves? Before we can trust even this seemingly obvious truth to be true, we must look beneath it to see if it has the bedrock support of an ultimate absolute. If we discover such an absolute, we need dig no deeper. We have reached the bedrock truth that must simply be accepted as a logical necessity or an unconditional standard too obvious to question.

Before we proceed, however, we must take a moment to address those who might question or deny that the preservation of society is a universally accepted tenet. One might say, "You won't find me stopping to help an injured motorist. I have my own life to live. Why should I be concerned with anyone else? Let that poor dude take care of himself." Yes, some people do think this way. Or at least, they try to. But almost always, when they fail to give help to someone in real need, they feel the stab of conscience.

The Sting of Guilt

I (Tom) remember an incident when my car battery died, leaving me stranded with my wife and three young daughters in a parking lot on a wintry day. I asked several passersby if they had jumper cables. Finally, one man admitted he did, but he didn't want to help us because he feared it might damage the alternator of his new car. He got in his vehicle to drive away, leaving us sitting in the cold. He sat there for a moment, then got out of the car, dug his cables from the trunk, and said, "I just can't drive away and leave you here. I'll help you."

A universal sense of right and wrong seems to be embedded within us, and we tend to measure our own actions by that innately sensed standard. When we fail to live up to that embedded standard, our conscience stings us just as it did the man with the jumper cables. We feel good when we do good to others, and we feel guilt when we fail to do it.

How, then, do we explain the German Nazis in the 1930s and 1940s? They seem to have felt no compulsion toward doing good. They were cruel, inhumane, and apparently immune to the sting of conscience. Their only guiding philosophy seemed to be the Nietzschean principle of power over others. Where was that innate sense of right and wrong within them?

In her book *The Nazi Conscience*, Claudia Koonz explains how the German people were incrementally conditioned to accept atrocities against the Jews among them. Using relentless and pervasive propaganda, Hitler convinced the Germans that their race was superior and it was their moral duty to maintain its purity. He simultaneously labeled the Jews among them as an inferior and dangerous race. The Nazis ensured acceptance of this propaganda by offering social and economic incentives to those who turned against their Jewish neighbors. Jobs, housing, goods, and professional opportunities opened up to those who complied, and once compliance began, rationalization took over and overrode their conscience.[2]

When the conscience is consistently overridden, it becomes stifled and inoperative, like a car's "check engine" light that's ignored so long it finally burns out. Those who bury their consciences, as did the Nazis, begin to operate without empathy or normal human feeling.

The striking thing to notice, however, is that those who live by such inhumane philosophies are never admired. Their actions are instinctively and universally censured as evil. In fact, the worst war in recorded history was fought to defeat the Nazis and their cohorts who defied the universally accepted moral code that urges humans to care for others. The widespread condemnation of those who step outside this code further demonstrates the presence of a universal sense of right and wrong embedded as an absolute truth within the human psyche—a sense so impelling that individuals and nations have made great sacrifices of life, wealth, and property to follow it.

Some claim this universal moral sense is embedded into humans through evolution. The obvious problem with this theory is that it contradicts a basic principle of evolution—the survival of the fittest. According to evolution, only the strong should survive to ensure the healthy continuation of the race. The weak and needy are unfit and will only impair the survival of the rest. Yet that universal moral sense operating within urges us to go out of our way to help the sick, the wounded, the underprivileged, and the deficient to survive.

Meet the Embedder

The bottom line is that the preservation of human life is a universally recognized principle so firmly embedded in the psyche of all sane humans in all societies throughout world history that we cannot help but believe it to be an authentic, baseline truth—an unconditional standard. This embedded truth strongly suggests the existence of an external "embedder" who planted truth within the human heart. Other explanations encounter obstacles that cannot be rationally overcome. (We will address these obstacles in chapter 5.) The answer that best fits the reality we experience is that the one who embedded this universal principle within humans is the supernatural being whom believers recognize as God.

At this point, we have reached bedrock. After determining the validity of our assumed truths by finding the greater truths they rest upon, we finally reach a truth that cannot be explained, because there is no greater truth beneath it. This is *bedrock truth*—the truth that must simply be assumed and accepted as a logical necessity because there is no rational alternative. It is the ultimate absolute for answering our deepest questions and giving meaning to everything we think and believe.

"Just a moment," you may say. "You have merely asserted the existence of God. You have not proved it." Of course we have not proved it. The ultimate absolute cannot be proved. If it could be proved, it would not be the ultimate absolute. Whatever you prove it by would be the ultimate absolute. That which cannot be proven can only be accepted or rejected. We maintain, however, that it should never be accepted or rejected blindly. Before we place our trust in God as the ultimate absolute, reason and preponderant evidence should show us that he is a logical necessity with no rational alternative. As we have shown above, there can be no other foundation solid enough to support a life filled with meaning and purpose. With God we reach bedrock, and it's time to start building.

Banishing Bedrock

Of course, you can choose not to assume that bedrock is solid. You can insist on empirical proof even where no such proof is possible. You can blast a hole in the bedrock to see how sturdy and dependable it really is, but then you ruin it as a basis for your foundation and must dig down to a deeper bedrock. If you consistently question and blast through each layer of rock you uncover, you will never have a foundation; you will merely have a hole in the ground. If you refuse to accept an ultimate absolute, you will never have a solid belief; you will merely have a hole in your life—that persistent feeling of emptiness and meaninglessness that haunts so many in our secular age.

This gnawing craving for meaning will persist until we accept the fact that there is something real out there that is beyond explanation and that explains everything else. This is why British author G. K. Chesterton compared God to the sun, saying, "The one created thing we cannot look at [the sun] is the one thing in the light of which we look at everything."[3] We must either accept the existence of this unproved absolute that underwrites objective truth or live with that inexplicable, nagging feeling that meaning and purpose should exist but do not. To put it another way, banishing God forces us to deny any possibility of satisfying that desire for meaning and purpose that persists in haunting us.

In the pervasive secularity of our age, we understand that many who long for meaning and purpose must overcome a natural resistance to accepting an unproved absolute. Postmodernity refuses to assume anything, while modernity demands rational proof for everything. As we have demonstrated, fulfilling this demand is a logical impossibility. Some unproved, foundational absolute must exist before anything at all can be proved. C. S. Lewis showed the futility of continuing to demand rational proof even at the foundation of one's belief:

> The kind of explanation which explains things away may give us something, though at a heavy cost. But you cannot go on "explaining away" for ever: you will find that you have explained explanation itself away. You cannot go on "seeing through" things for ever. . . . It is good that the window should be transparent, because the street or garden beyond it is opaque. How if you saw through the garden too? It is no use trying to "see through" first principles. If you see through everything, then everything is transparent. But a wholly transparent world is an invisible world. To "see through" all things is the same as not to see.[4]

Before we can believe anything at all, we must accept the existence of a bedrock principle so opaque that we can't see through it.

In this chapter we have introduced God as the only viable bedrock absolute for building a life foundation that accords with reality as we experience it. In subsequent chapters we will expand on what we have established here. We will show how belief in God is the only way we can validate the reality we experience in various areas of life. To put it another way, we will demonstrate how belief in God provides the only possible foundation for building a life of meaning and purpose.

QUESTIONS FOR THOUGHT AND DISCUSSION

1. What practical functions do standards serve in our world?

2. What is the difference between conditional standards and unconditional standards?

3. What do you mean when you use the term *truth*?

4. Do truth and morality need standards to validate their authenticity? Explain.

5. Do you think meaning and purpose are realities or illusions? Explain.

6. Why do so many people resist the idea of authentic truth and morality as presented in this chapter?

7. What rationales will people use to get around the Christian view of authentic truth and morality? What is your view of authentic truth and morality after reading this chapter? Has it changed?

THE TROUBLESOME
WALL OF REALITY

Is it possible to create our own workable version of truth?

The late composer John Cage found the laws that govern the composition of music too restrictive. By discarding standard musical forms, he produced what he called "indeterminate" performance pieces that relied almost solely on random sounds produced by chance. One of Cage's pieces, titled "4'33"," consists of an onstage orchestra or pianist doing nothing for four minutes and thirty-three seconds, while the only sounds in the auditorium are those produced randomly by the audience—shuffling, coughing, whispering, rattling programs, etc. The point of the piece is that if we shut down sources that deliberately manipulate sound to please the ear or communicate a feeling (the orchestra or piano), we learn to appreciate sound in its natural state (random noises arising from natural sources).

In another John Cage piece titled "Inlets," performers use conch shells filled with water. Tilting the shells creates a bubble inside, which produces a sound at chance intervals. Cage's "Imaginary Landscapes No. 4" consists of twelve radios with their dials randomly turned throughout the piece by twenty-four performers. Many of his compositions deliberately give the performers incomplete written instructions with no musical notations, instead leaving them to figure out what to do onstage.

The laws that govern the composition of music were not invented; they were discovered. Early composers struggling to create meaningful music learned by experimentation what combinations of notes produced harmony or dissonance and how intervals, rests, dynamics, and the duration of tones could evoke emotion and drama. Over the centuries, these musical laws have been codified, and they are now recognized as valid because they correspond to the way the human ear and brain process sound. Today they comprise the standard by which music is composed.

John Cage, however, tried to create an alternate musical reality in which randomness and chance sounds are presented as being superior to harmonically composed music. He contended that the deliberate communication of an idea or feeling is an invalid use of music—that composed music restricts sound, which according to Cage is meant to be organically produced. Francis Schaeffer noted that the randomness of Cage's music was a deliberate expression of his belief that the universe itself is random and operates by sheer chance.

Cage was strongly influenced by Chinese Zen philosophy as presented in the *I Ching*, which outlines systems to produce randomness that would aid the mind in obtaining oracles from pantheistic deities. The difference, as Schaeffer pointed out, was that "as far as Cage is concerned, there is nobody there to speak. There is only an impersonal universe speaking through blind chance."[1]

John Cage was also a connoisseur of mushrooms. When he wandered the woods near his home, he always carried his handy copy of *Field Guide to Mushrooms*.[2] Why did Cage need a guide to picking mushrooms? Why didn't he pick them with the same freedom he employed in composing music? Cage, knowing that some species of mushrooms contain deadly poison, explained, "I became aware that if I approached mushrooms in the spirit of my chance operations, I would die shortly. So I decided that I would not approach them in that way!"[3]

As we can see, John Cage lived in two separate worlds that operated by diametrically opposing philosophies. One was a world of chance and disorder, the other a world of strict order. His musical world, through which he expressed his philosophy of life, consisted entirely of his self-constructed reality, which flouted the tested realities of musical composition and relied solely on chance. Yet when he stepped outside his musical fantasyland into the world where wrong decisions could be fatal, he banished chance in favor of deliberate and calculated actions based on realities to which he had to conform. Because Cage lived in two irreconcilable worlds, his life was not *integrated*, which is to say it lacked integrity.

Almost everyone enjoys stepping outside reality into a fantasy world now and then. That's why Disneyland, Universal Studios, video games, and sci-fi and fantasy books and movies are so popular. But indulging in an alternate reality as an occasional diversion is altogether different from promoting it as an existential truth, as John Cage did. His alternative music was a philosophical statement asserting that chance and chaos are natural realities, while order and harmony confine and limit and deprive us of freedom.

Alas for Mr. Cage, he apparently didn't realize that his compartmentalized life actually undermined his stated philosophy. He demonstrated that we cannot survive in a life lived by an adopted reality in which no human will is imposed on nature and chance is allowed to reign supreme. The only reality in which we can survive is the old, inconvenient reality of rigid law, which has been demanded by the nature of the universe since its beginning.

The Inconsistencies of Alternative Truths

The music of John Cage demonstrates one of the primary problems that comes with the secular world's banishment of God. It is the difficulty in living an integrated life where all facets of our existence conform to a unified reality. In today's postmodern world, it is commonly believed that we are granted the right to construct our own reality. Whatever you believe about yourself or your environment should be considered true for you. Yet those who construct alternate realities inevitably find them out of step with the reality they encounter in everyday life.

For example, a biological woman is now granted the right to be considered a man despite her female anatomy and attributes—and society is expected to endorse her choice. This becomes her "truth," her "reality." Nonetheless, she will find this chosen truth challenged at every turn. Though others may accede to her wishes and address her as Robert instead of Roberta, they will inevitably think of her as a woman or at least as something less than a complete and authentic man. Even the most politically correct people will have to carefully monitor themselves to uphold her choice, remembering the right pronouns, forcing their senses to disregard the obvious discrepancies, and making allowances for areas in which her "truth" clashes with the rights of others— as in the use of restrooms and dressing facilities. Even if over time society becomes inured to these incongruities and takes them in stride, practical discrepancies will persist. Success in men's sports will be impossible for her. She will not qualify for jobs requiring a man's physical strength. Half the fixtures in men's restrooms will not accommodate her anatomy, unless she chooses to undergo significant surgery. She will never beget a child in the way a biological man would. Her chosen reality will always clash with preexisting reality. Even if she undergoes surgery and hormonal treatment to give her body the appearance of a male, every one of her thirty trillion cells will continue to carry the genetic code of a female.

The reason for this dissonance is simple: the real universe is too relentlessly rational and orderly to allow us to construct workable versions of our own reality that mesh naturally with preexisting reality. Every day we will be forced to contend with true realities that cannot be denied or avoided.

Why, then, do postmodernists construct their own realities? According to philosophy professor Stephen Hicks, head of the Center for Ethics and Entrepreneurship at Rockford University, it is because existing reality does not accord with their wishes. As Dr. Hicks put it, "What the major postmodernists are talking about is being free from reason, being free from reality, being free from the constraints of human nature, denying that facts about reality and human nature should ground values and determine the choices we make."[4]

This, no doubt, explains why postmodernism—though widely accepted in the humanities departments of universities and as a personal philosophy—has never become the driving engine of today's secular culture. Invention, manufacturing, shipping, communication, and the technologies driving commerce depend on the rational certainties of cause and effect, premise and conclusion, experiment and verification, inference and deduction. Yet many who must necessarily exclude postmodernism from their workaday world choose to indulge it as a personal philosophy. Dr. Hicks expressed this contradictory, two-level split in this way:

We know it is possible for individuals to
compartmentalize themselves psychologically in
fairly dramatic ways. And we know, for example,
that a practicing scientist may, outside of the lab,
profess mystical, irrational, religious beliefs. But once
he goes into the lab, all of that is left outside. In the
lab, he functions objectively and in a reality-oriented
fashion.[5]

Salvo magazine reported that in a Twitter post in the summer of 2020, teacher and PhD student Brittany Marshall
asserted that the basic mathematical equation $2 + 2 = 4$ "is
cultural and because of western imperialism/colonization, we
think of it as the only way of knowing."[6] Another teacher
chimed in, tweeting, "Standards aren't objective. That's the
whole point. Math isn't objective either. It's always down to
interpretation."[7]

We can be pretty sure that these postmodernists do not
follow their nonobjective philosophy about math when fig-
uring their checkbooks or when measuring dosages for medicines, tablespoons for cooking, or window sizes for drapery.
When at work, on the job, or in the lab, few people can
be true postmodernists. Even Silicon Valley executives are
forced to rely on objective reason and fixed mathematics as
they create new electronic devices and work out the bugs.
When they close shop in the evening, however, many shed
the chafing strictures of reality like overstarched shirts and

live as postmodernists, discarding all guiding principles but the philosophy of doing what feels good.

As Dr. Hicks points out, having this irrational contradiction buttressed by a recognized philosophy gives postmodernists "a get-out-of-jail-free card against any rational attack on [their] system."[8] Like composer John Cage, who lived in a world of fantasy with his compositions and the world of reality with his mushrooms, their lives lack integrity. They are not integrated into a consistent alignment with reality. In the world of necessity, objective reality reigns and postmodernism evaporates. This fact speaks volumes about human recognition of the nature of reality. We may use postmodernism as a justification for dismissing reality when it conflicts with our desires, but in areas where it is necessary to comply with the way the world works, we are forced to cling to experiential reality, just as humanity has done throughout history.

Is the Appearance of Design a Reality or an Illusion?

Evolutionary biologist Richard Dawkins believes that nature itself projects an illusion that does not conform to reality. On the first page of his book *The Blind Watchmaker*, he writes, "Biology is the study of complicated things that give the appearance of having been designed for a purpose."[9] Later in the book he adds, "We may say that a living body or organ is well designed if it has attributes that an intelligent and knowledgeable engineer might have built into it in order to achieve some sensible purpose. . . . [A]ny engineer can recognize an object that has been designed, even poorly designed, for a purpose, and he can usually work out what that purpose is just by looking at the structure of the object."[10] Here Dawkins seems to recognize that design and purpose are paired necessities. Purpose requires design.

The primary point of Dawkins's book, however, is to convince us that despite what he admits to be the overwhelming appearance of design in nature, that appearance is an illusion. He insists that everything in existence came about through random, mindless, and accidental processes. Although the eye appears to have been designed for sight, it came into existence via blind chance. While feet seem to be designed for locomotion, hands for working, stomachs for digesting, and genitals for reproducing, according to Dawkins, all these organs and limbs came about through random, unplanned, natural processes.

Dawkins and other scientists claim to be objective in their pursuit of truth. They place great stress on following the evidence wherever it leads. By Dawkins's own admission, the appearance of design in all the forms of the universe suggests the existence of a superintelligent designer. Yet he rejects this appearance of design as valid evidence of it and spends all his considerable skill and energy defending the opposite conclusion.

It seems to us that an objective mind would consider the appearance of design as possible evidence that should be followed wherever it leads. The refusal of Dawkins and others to follow this evidence undercuts their claim to scientific objectivity. If we follow the evidence offered by appearance, isn't it possible that we might find that true reality corresponds with the way it presents itself?

Is Free Will a Reality or an Illusion?

In another of his books, *The Selfish Gene*, Dawkins reveals what he believes humans to be: "We are survival machines—robot vehicles blindly programmed to preserve the selfish molecules known as genes. . . . we, and all other animals, are machines created by our genes."[11] Here Dawkins tells us that since we were created not by a designer but by nature, we are merely machines—robots moved about and manipulated by the natural drives and impulses programmed into us.

I'm sure you have seen videos of amazing robots that can walk, jump, pick up objects, sense and avoid obstacles, keep their balance when pushed or hit, and get up by themselves when they fall. We know that these incredible machines have no options in choosing their behavior. They merely do as their programs direct and make automatic adjustments in response to built-in sensors attuned to their external environment. This, according to Dawkins, describes the nature of humans. We are nothing more than highly complex and immeasurably more elaborate programmed robots with every action dictated by the software in our brain, which is really nothing more than a highly sophisticated computer.

If Dawkins is correct, it means we humans have no real

behavior options. We make no real choices. What seem to be choices are really actions predetermined by our computer brains responding automatically to data fed into them by the senses. We make no decisions and need no guidance in choosing our actions and responses. Our cranial program dictates everything we do.

The term for this naturalistic* philosophy of human activity is *determinism*. Determinism says that all our actions are predetermined even before we commit them. We have no capacity for choice. Everything we do is as inevitable as the trajectory of a billiard ball when struck at a given angle with given force. Determinism is the natural outgrowth of evolution. It is essentially a principle of Newtonian physics—every action generates an equal and opposite reaction—applied to human behavior.

Determinism tells us that while programming our brains to dictate all our actions and responses, nature played a strange little trick on us. It hid from our consciousness all awareness of the automaton we are and gave us the illusion of choice. When the central idea of Dawkins's book came into his mind, he felt as if he had thought of it himself and chose to do the research and begin writing. But if his philosophy of determinism is correct, these choices were merely illusions. Hundreds or thousands of impulses accumulated

---

* To remind you of what we noted in the foreword, when we use the terms *naturalism* or *naturalistic*, we mean the philosophy which asserts that nature is all that exists; that there is no supernatural realm; and that there is no transcendent God who exists outside or above nature. There may be shades of difference between naturalism, materialism, secularism, and atheism, but for brevity and simplicity we will use *naturalism* as a convenient term to encompass these and similar beliefs that exclude God.

through his senses and compelled him to write his book. These impulses could have been activated by events such as a confrontation with a Christian, an article about synaptic impulses, a speech on determinism—all of which combined to produce an impulse in his brain that compelled a thought to come into his consciousness in the form of a choice: "I believe I'll consider writing a book about this." But according to Dawkins's deterministic philosophy, that conscious thought was a deceptive facade. The data accumulated in his brain had already determined that his physical organism would respond by writing the book. He could no more help but do it than a robot could refuse to carry out its programmed instructions.

If determinism is the true reality, we should never feel the urgings of conscience. According to strict naturalism, conscience and guilt are meaningless concepts. If all our actions are determined automatically, we have no control over them, which means that conscience, which prods us to make moral choices, should not exist. Determinism says we are incapable of making choices, moral or otherwise. Nor should we ever feel the sting of guilt that comes from violating the conscience. It makes no sense for a machine to have feelings of guilt when every action it performs is mechanistic and inevitable.

Here is where naturalists themselves encounter their first problem with determinism—a practical problem. In his book *The Moral Animal*, science writer Robert Wright concludes that free will is "an illusion, brought to us by evolution."[12]

Yet he understands that to openly adopt determinism as our operating philosophy would destroy society. Although environment, heredity, and biochemistry determine every human action, we need to believe we have free will because determinism destroys society's ability to maintain order, law, and justice by eroding blame for destructive behavior. When a person commits murder, how can society justify arresting and punishing him when a robotic machine cannot help but do what a machine does?

The late theoretical physicist Stephen Hawking was aware of this problem. He also was a strong proponent of determinism, defending the concept in several of his books. In *The Grand Design* (written with Leonard Mlodinow), Hawking states that "free will is just an illusion."[13] Yet in an essay titled "Is Everything Determined?" he says that while the universe is deterministic, to survive we are forced to act as if it is not. We must act as if we have free will. Though he believed all human actions were determined by a grand unified theory, he writes,

> If the theory has determined that we shall die by hanging, then we shall not drown. But you would have to be awfully sure that you were destined for the gallows to put to sea in a small boat during a storm. I have noticed that even people who claim that everything is predestined and that we can do nothing to change it look before they cross the road. . . . One cannot base one's conduct on the idea that

everything is determined, because one does not
know what has been determined. Instead, one has
to adopt the effective theory that one has free will
and that one is responsible for one's actions.[14]

Yes, the universe is deterministic, says Hawking, but the
only way to survive is to live as if it is not, because we do not
know what has been determined. Like other naturalists, he
believes we must disregard the reality demanded by naturalism and live by what he sees as the illusion of free will.

In the same essay, Hawking says, "Our intelligence, our
ability to draw the correct conclusions from the information
provided by our sense organs, must date back to our cave
dweller days or earlier. It would have been selected for on
the basis of our ability to kill certain animals for food and to
avoid being killed by other animals."[15] Here he tells us that
nature enables us to survive by perceiving reality, whereas in
the case of determinism he tells us that the only way to survive is to ignore reality. Do you detect a bit of inconsistency
here? It is inevitable, for it is impossible for determinists (or
naturalists or postmodernists) to remain consistent with their
philosophy.

The reality asserted by determinism clashes with the reality we experience. All of us feel as if we make real choices.
It's very likely that you yourself have agonized over monumental alternatives. *Shall I take the job in another town or stay
and let my daughter finish high school? Shall I install a new
transmission or buy a new car? Should I marry Richard despite*

his temper? It often seems our future happiness hangs in the balance. After sleepless agonizing, we finally make the hard decision, which sometimes leads to good results and sometimes does not. This universal experience makes it very hard to deny that what appears to be true *is* true: we humans do indeed make free choices.

Canadian philosopher Charles Taylor points out that one of the ways modern secularists are urged to validate themselves and find meaning is to make choices. As he puts it, for the secularist it is about "bare choice as a prime value, irrespective of what it is a choice between, or in what domain."[16] Here Taylor amplifies the contradiction built into naturalistic philosophies. On the one hand, the secularist is to validate himself by making choices. But on the other hand, his deterministic philosophy forces him to believe that free choice does not exist.

The contradictions inherent in naturalistic philosophy begin to pile up. Naturalism requires us to deny too many apparent realities as illusions and yet to live as if those illusions are true.

Is the Human Conscience a Reality or an Illusion?

In C. S. Lewis's novel *That Hideous Strength*, the naturalistic scientist Professor Frost believes himself to be nothing more than a machine that functions via determinism. He is aware, resentfully, of the presence of an internal voice that seems to stand above the machine he claims to be. This voice keeps up a running commentary on all his activities and makes unwelcome judgments about his decisions and actions. Frost denies the reality of this voice, insisting it is an illusion, a phantom projected by his consciousness. He has worked hard to silence the voice and base all action solely on automatic responses appropriate to the machine he thinks he is. The ultimate horror descends on Frost as he faces sudden death. In that instant he realizes this voice has been the expression of his free self, his conscience. It was never an illusion or a mere appearance; it was a true reality.[17]

Lewis, like other theists, was convinced that the human conscience is a reality—a monitor of behavior, designed to help humans align their choices with the absolute standards of morality. Reality affirms what Christians believe—that the conscience and the morality it asserts are embedded in the human soul by the transcendent God of the universe.

Naturalistic philosophy necessarily denies the existence of the conscience. If we are machines created by evolution and driven by robotics, we have no need of a conscience. Distinguishing between right and wrong is meaningless if humans are purely mechanistic. Yet most recognize the presence of something within us that acts much like a conscience. Psychologist Eric Fromm explains this phenomenon as a sense of fear externally imposed on us as we learn and develop. According to Fromm, this sense is not embedded by a god; it is created by authority figures, such as a father or a religious leader who plants within us at impressionable ages a fear of disobedience that emerges as guilt when we violate rules imposed on us.[18]

Sigmund Freud saw conscience as an internalized father figure looming over our decisions and creating guilt feelings when our behavior deviates from what we've been taught.[19] Friedrich Nietzsche defined the conscience as a reactive mechanism learned from social experience. It prods us to toe the prescribed line to avoid punishment or unpleasant outcomes.[20]

In the reality created by naturalists, what we call conscience is merely a collection of ideas about right and wrong devised by authority figures and religions and driven into our brains by repetition similar to brainwashing. This invasive moral sense makes us feel guilty when we violate the behavior it prescribes. But if we would just realize that we are nothing more than survival machines, say the naturalists, we would see that neither conscience nor guilt belong in our makeup.

The conscience, however, exhibits several characteristics that defy naturalistic claims to its being an illusion.

The Conscience Demands Ultimate Obedience

First, the conscience demands ultimate obedience. Even in our day of disrespect for authority, most people, including secularists, say we should be true to conscience. French Enlightenment philosopher Voltaire said, "The safest course is to do nothing against one's conscience."[21] According to novelist Joseph Conrad, "All a man can betray is his conscience."[22]

Agnostic author Robert G. Ingersoll asserted that "courage without conscience is a wild beast."[23] Contemporary Indian actress Parvathy said, "My career strategy has never been the most important thing, my conscience is."[24] Obeying your conscience is often equated with being true to yourself. As Polonius advised Laertes in Shakespeare's *Hamlet*, "This above all: to thine own self be true, and it must follow, as the night the day, thou canst not then be false to any man."[25] To be true to ourselves is to act in accord with that internal guiding voice that theists identify as conscience and secularists claim is a culturally created illusion. If it is an illusion, why do naturalists think it so important to remain true to its dictates?

The Conscience Surprises with Judgments That Were Not Taught

A second validation of conscience is that it can surprise us with judgments about behaviors we were not taught. In an *Esquire* article, Dr. Richard Selzer writes of witnessing his first abortion. Not being religious, he had no convictions about the morality of abortion. He expected it to be a routine, clinical procedure. But Selzer was shocked at what he saw. After the fatal chemical was injected through the mother's abdomen into her uterus, the needle suddenly jerked about as the baby convulsed, squirmed, kicked, and flailed to avoid the pain. Selzer was horrified. He suddenly realized that in that room, at that moment, there existed two radically different worlds. The first was the world of the physician and his

attending clinicians, who were calmly carrying out a technical procedure they viewed as routine business. The second
world existed inside that dark womb, where an innocent,
sentient being was suddenly seared with extreme pain and
was fighting for her very life.

At the end of the article, Selzer writes: "You cannot reason
with me now. For what can language do against the truth of
what I saw?"[26] A sudden sense of right and wrong that he had
never considered suddenly invaded Dr. Selzer's being. His
conscience told him something he had never been taught,
something so profoundly true that neither words nor reason
could unseat it. It was a truth that nature alone could not
have supplied.

The Conscience Often Contradicts Nature

A third validation of the reality of conscience is that it often
contradicts nature. In his book *The Moral Animal*, Robert
Wright dismissed the idea of humans having a built-in guide
to right and wrong. As he put it, "'Moral guidance' is a euphe-
mism."[27] Like other naturalists, he believes what we refer to
as conscience is the seat of what we call moral behavior, but
it is really a survival mechanism that evolved with the species.

The problem with this theory, which we will explore more
fully in chapter 5, is that the conscience asks us to perform
in ways that have nothing to do with the survival of our own
genes or even of the species in general. Conscience asks us to
help even those who cannot perpetuate the species but in fact

weaken it. Nurses, doctors, friends, and even strangers feel an internal call to assist weak, sick, unstable, and dying people who are not capable of surviving on their own. They often do it at risk of their own lives. The strong risking themselves for the weak contradicts evolutionary theory and strongly suggests that conscience could not have arisen from within nature.

Our own personal experience with conscience shows it to be an embedded presence too powerful to stifle. Denying its existence will not make it go away. Conscience affects both theists and naturalists alike. We feel guilty when we lie or steal. We are appalled at ourselves when we lose our temper and hurt a loved one. We can't live with bearing the blame for our misdeeds, so we make excuses to justify our bad behavior.

Even psychopaths who do not seem to have a conscience cannot stand to bear blame or guilt. The most hardened criminals offer rationales for their crimes: they were mistreated or deprived as children; society has cheated them, and they are evening the score; their victims deserved what they got.

Those who operate outside the universal moral code will always grope for traditional morality to justify their errant behavior. They saw off the limb they sit on and then grab the trunk to keep from falling. Sane people cannot live at peace with themselves without finding some way, whether real or contrived, to justify their behavior by the standard the universe prescribes. If the universe really is meaningless and humans are nothing more than organic robots, we should not need to scramble for excuses. Yet we do. We all feel compelled to align ourselves with the universal standard of morality. This is true even of those who deny such a standard. Their behavior affirms the very reality they deny. If they fail to justify themselves by that standard, the conscience they deny will sting them just as painfully as that of the theists.

Just as the existence of the eye implies light, the existence of the conscience implies God. But in a naturalistic universe, the conscience that serves as a monitor of moral behavior is unnecessary, unwelcome, and inexplicable.

The Futility of Escaping Reality

In this chapter we have shown that naturalists must deny apparent reality in many areas to maintain their belief in a naturalistic universe:

- While the universe has the appearance of design, in their reality design is an illusion.
- While we seem to have free will, in their reality free will is an illusion.
- While we seem to have a conscience, in their reality conscience is an illusion.

In these and many other areas, naturalists must continually assert that reality is the opposite of what it seems. Yet they admit that to survive and flourish, we must live our lives according to the illusion of reality rather than by what they claim reality to be.

Is it possible that naturalists may have their realities inverted? Isn't it possible that the reality that they admit *appears* to be real might actually *be* real? If to survive we must live by what they claim is an illusion of reality, isn't it possible that it is not an illusion after all? Naturalists must maintain that apparent reality is an illusion because if they admitted it to be true, it would open the door to the existence of God—a door they insist must remain closed. Among scientists who claim to follow the evidence wherever it leads, why is the option of an intelligent designer automatically placed off the table? Why must the evidence of appearance be ruled out? If it looks like a duck, walks like a duck, quacks like a duck, flies like a duck, and swims like a duck, why isn't it possible that it just might indeed be a duck?

Postmodernists may deny the reality of solid, absolute truth and insist that human minds are incapable of reaching any true conclusions, but they still believe the conclusions of their own thinking. When they claim there is no absolute truth, they must at least believe that claim to be absolutely true, which saddles them with yet another contradiction. To put it another way, *they must believe their thinking is true even when it leads them to conclude there can be no truth*—and they must find some way to cope with the inconsistency of this conclusion.

The realities of existence that spring from the very nature of the universe force postmodernists and naturalists to live and think in ways that are inconsistent with their philosophies. Choosing to believe that conscience, morality, free will, and truth do not exist does not make naturalists immune to their effects. Many today want to think that whatever they choose to believe becomes real for them. But reality grants no exemptions. Deciding a hot stove is cold will not keep it from burning the hand that touches it.

The examples we have presented in this chapter show that the universe demonstrates true realities that will not accommodate human-constructed alternate realities. True reality is so unyielding that no alternate can be sustained indefinitely. We believe that the reality of the universe is founded on absolute truth, and all alternative realities are fabrications with no real existence. Anything that is not true is merely the noise of a moment, a dying echo that reveals its hollowness against the unmoving walls of true reality.

QUESTIONS FOR THOUGHT AND DISCUSSION

1. Why did the life of composer John Cage lack integrity? (Clue: notice the resemblance of the words "integrity" and "integrated.")

2. Why isn't it possible to construct one's own workable version of truth or reality?

3. Why do naturalists admit that the universe appears to have been designed but deny that it was?

4. How can you know that you are not a naturalistic robot?

5. Why is naturalism's denial of conscience inconsistent with reality? In what ways have you felt compelled to align yourself with conscience or a sense of morality?

6. Explain determinism. Why doesn't it resonate with the reality we experience?

7. How do we know that free will is a reality and not an illusion?

4

THE ELEPHANT
IN THE ROOM

*Does individual subjectivity
undermine our ability to reason?*

A story is told of a man who was afflicted with a strange form
of insanity. He thought he was dead. His friends and family
used every evidence and means of logic they could think of
to convince him that he was alive. "You breathe, you eat, you
talk, you think," they said. "All your senses are working; you
see, hear, smell, feel, and taste." When these explanations
had no effect, they pointed out that he moved about and
functioned like a living person. They pinched him, and he
felt pain. He experienced emotions of happiness and sadness.
Yet all proofs fell flat. Nothing anyone said changed the man's
mind. He was sure he was dead.

Finally, a friend came up with what he thought was
certain proof to convince the man that he was alive. "You
realize that dead men don't bleed, don't you?" The afflicted

man admitted it was true: dead men don't bleed. His friend quickly grabbed the man's hand and, with his pocketknife, pricked his finger.

The man stared wide-eyed and utterly amazed as red blood seeped from the little wound. "Well, what do you know," he said, awe reflected in his voice, "I never would have guessed it. Dead men *do* bleed."

The poor man was so immersed in his own version of reality that he forced even an obvious truth to bend to it.

How can we be certain that what we *think* is really *true*—whether it conforms to reality? One of the first thinkers to address this question was the seventeenth-century French philosopher René Descartes. He wondered how it's possible to prove the truth of anything at all. Could we be mistaken even about the most obvious of apparent realities, which is our own existence? Do I really exist as an objective being, or is my belief that I exist merely an illusion?

Descartes finally came up with an answer—his famous *cogito, ergo sum.* "I think, therefore I am." With this premise and conclusion, he asserted that his ability to question his existence was a proof of it. He reasoned that the experience of conscious thought could not occur unless he existed as an objective being capable of producing the thought.

We sometimes wonder at the tendency of philosophers to formulate propositions about facts that seem too obvious to question. Wasn't Descartes's mirror enough to prove he existed? His quest makes more sense than may appear at first blush. As we noted in chapter 2, no belief is beyond question unless it has the support of a solid foundation. Descartes reasoned that his ability to think was foundation enough to prove that his existence was an objective reality.

Humans have used reason to reach conclusions throughout recorded history. Ancient philosophers such as Socrates, Aristotle, and Plato and eighteenth-century Enlightenment philosophers such as Locke, Hume, and Kant have strongly influenced the modern Western world with their elevation of reason as the primary guide to truth. They believed that by the power of reason alone, humankind could eventually come to know all truth and create an earthly utopia.

Most of us think little about our ability to reason. We merely take it for granted. We use reason every day to interpret and process facts about our world, especially facts that may not be immediately apparent to the senses. For example, you may remember when a grade school teacher first showed your class a geographic globe and told you the world is round. The claim seemed unbelievable because everywhere around you the earth appears to be flat. You wondered what kept people in Australia from falling off into space. The teacher taught you to validate this truth by observing facts such as sunrises, sunsets, gravity, the disappearance of ships sailing over the horizon, and the way stars seem to move across the nighttime sky. Applying reason to these evidences led you to accept the teacher's claim about the shape of the earth.

Reason leads us to accept truths that we could not know except by exercising the rational faculties of our mind. By the use of reason, we make inferences and form conclusions about the nature of reality that guide us in our everyday lives.

The Postmodern Rejection of Reason

Somewhere around the last quarter of the twentieth century, the philosophy of postmodernism arose to question all truth claims and the methods by which we attempt to discern reality. Postmodernists assert that reason is undependable as a means of discovering truth. They tell us that personal experiences, cultural indoctrination, biases, desires, preconceptions, conditioning, mental disorders, and flawed information hopelessly skew the process of reason. Like the man who thought he was dead, we deceive ourselves when we believe we are thinking rationally. Our inevitable subjectivity undermines all attempts to find objective truth.

To show that reason is fatally flawed, postmodernists sometimes employ the well-known illustration of several blind men describing an elephant. As you may remember, the blind man who stood behind the elephant felt only its tail and reasoned that elephants are like ropes. The man standing beside the elephant felt only its side and claimed that elephants are like walls. The man who felt its leg insisted that elephants are like trees. The man at the front of the animal grasped its trunk and asserted that elephants are like large snakes. Each man formed a conclusion based on the evidence at hand, but those conclusions did not yield the truth about an elephant.

According to postmodernists, this story reveals the fatal flaw in reason. Reason is not a dependable tool for discerning truth because our personal perspectives and the narrowness of our individual viewpoints and experiences distort our perception and blind us to anything we might call reality.

As we study the illustration more closely, however, we can see that the elephant story actually proves the opposite of the postmodern claim. Reason does lead to truth. Each blind man did indeed find a truth about the elephant, though it differed from the truths discovered by his peers. The problem was simply that none of these individual truths added up to the whole truth. The failure of the blind men was not a failure of *reason*; it was a failure of *reasoning*. What the men postulated about an elephant would have been true enough had their claims been more modest. The elephant's *tail*—not the entire elephant—is indeed like a rope, its *side* is like a wall, and its *legs* are like trees. Each man described accurately enough the limited part of reality he encountered. The mistake was in drawing conclusions too broad to be supported by such limited data.

The limitations of the blind men's personal viewpoints need not have kept them from knowing more of the truth than they discovered for themselves. They could have communicated with each other, shared their experiences, and even exchanged places to broaden their limited viewpoints and collect more data. Had they taken these steps, their combined knowledge could easily have brought them quite close to the objective truth about the shape of an elephant. Each tried to infer the entire elephant from an insufficient sampling of evidence. The men applied reason poorly and got poor results.

Reason is not discredited by poor usage any more than Beethoven's music is discredited by poor performances. Because distortions of reason can lead to false conclusions, postmodernists choose not to trust it. The veteran watchdog sometimes barks at shadows, so it is muzzled to keep it from barking at all, leaving the gate of gullibility unguarded.

The postmodern assertion that we are incapable of finding real truth leads to the unjustified claim that varied versions of truth are equally valid. With absolute truth unknowable or nonexistent, postmodernists claim the best we can do is to allow our personal view of reality to be the truth we adopt for ourselves.

If we allow the assertions shaped by personal biases, conditioning, and preconceptions to be called "this person's truth" or "that person's truth," it means the word *truth* has no content. If everyone's varying perception of truth is equally valid, then truth is a meaningless term. A word that can mean anything means nothing—and this is close to what the postmodernists are telling us. Because of their perceived difficulty in affirming truth, they assert truth to be an empty concept with no objective meaning.

This claim overlooks something glaringly obvious: there is a real elephant in the postmodernist's room. The blind men's hands were feeling a reality that was objectively there. Otherwise, it could not have been felt at all. To state it another way, *the truth about an elephant exists objectively even if no one apprehends it accurately.* Misunderstandings about reality have no effect whatsoever on reality itself. The blind men's failure to reason their way to the truth about an elephant did not do away with the elephant. Denying or ignoring this fact is at the core of the postmodern error in dealing with reason and truth.

By denying the possibility of objective reasoning, postmodernists leave themselves no basis for believing in postmodernism. Their claim that reason cannot lead to truth collapses any rationale for believing postmodernism to be true. They assert that all human thought is too flawed to apprehend truth—except for the one thought that says postmodernism is true. But if all thought collapses, so must this one. Postmodernism pulls the chair out from under itself.

Is Human Reason Dependable?

Having uncovered the fatal weakness of postmodernism, we must now turn around and ask: How can we be sure that reason is dependable? How do we know the postmodernists are wrong in claiming that reason is a flawed and unreliable function of the brain that we mistakenly believe to be a valid path to truth? Can we find any kind of bedrock for reason that guarantees its dependability?

The need to question reason hardly occurs to most of us. Reason is a product of our thinking brains, and our thought processes seem to conform to the reality we experience.

Mathematics, for example, which requires abstract reasoning, can be verified by actual experience in the tangible world. We don't have to depend solely on the internal workings of our minds or fear the intrusion of our biases to know that two plus two always equals four. We can verify our internal reasoning with an external experiment. We can place two oranges on the table, count them carefully, and then place two more beside them and count again. Voilà! Our senses confirm what we reasoned abstractly in our minds. Just as we hypothesized, we do indeed have four oranges. Abstract reasoning and experiential reality seem to coincide.

Nevertheless, the question persists. How do we know that either our internal thinking or the reality we perceive is objective and rational? How do we know that the teacher mentioned in the previous chapter who dismissed mathematics as a culturally imposed standard is not right? How do we know those oranges are not figments of our imagination or that mathematics is anything more than a trick of our brains? How do we know our minds are not misfiring like that of the man who thought he was dead? The thinking of a person with a mental illness seems utterly rational to him. His experience of external reality conforms to his skewed internal thinking. A man who thinks he is Napoleon finds his belief confirmed in every word, every event, every circumstance of his existence. Strike up a friendly conversation about the weather, and he may suspect you of being a spy for General Wellington trying to trick him into revealing whether he is planning an attack if it doesn't rain. A mentally ill person interprets reality through the filter of his illness and has no clue that his thinking is skewed.

Even generally sane minds may experience distortions they cannot recognize. These distortions may be produced by permanent preconditioning, by ongoing influences, or by temporary factors. For example, the story is told of a writer (often said to be nineteenth-century American psychologist/ philosopher William James) who sometimes experimented with hallucinogens to alter his mental state. He was convinced that under the influence of these drugs, his thoughts became extraordinarily profound and insightful. To record those mental gems, he kept a pencil in hand as he dosed himself. When he emerged from the drug's influence, he found that he had written, "Hogamus, higamus, men are polygamous; higamus, hogamus, women—monogamous." Obviously, the hallucinogen not only confounded the man's rationality; it also skewed his judgment and left him in no condition to know it.[1]

How do we know all human brains are not as permanently confused as this writer's was temporarily? How do we know whether we are thinking rational thoughts about a rational universe, or whether we are all confined to an asylum where every thought is an illusion that seems rational only to ourselves? When we try to prove the validity of reason, this is the dilemma we face. It is impossible to prove by reasoning that human reason is dependable, for when reason is in question, its own claim to be valid is meaningless. When the accused is also the judge, the verdict cannot be trusted. We can't expect reason to testify against itself. This means we cannot prove the reliability of reason simply by reasoning. Yet if we are uncertain about reason, we must question our capacity to be certain about anything at all.

If we left the question there, it might seem that the post-modernists are right after all in claiming knowledge of absolute truth to be beyond our grasp. Yet when we compare the only two possible options for the source of reason—naturalism or a supernatural intelligence—a solid answer begins to emerge. Let's consider how reason stands up as the product of either of these two options.

Naturalism as the Source of Human Reason

As we have noted several times, today's secular and post-modern view of reality is shaped by the philosophy of naturalism, which asserts that nature is all there is. According to naturalists, there is no supernatural realm outside the natural universe—no transcendent creative intelligence and no whisper of Charles Taylor's supernatural enchantment. Naturalists believe everything that exists came into being accidentally, without the agency of a supernatural first cause. Through a mindless process without plan or purpose, particles formed into atoms, atoms into molecules, molecules into inorganic structures, and inorganic structures into lifeforms. From within certain life-forms emerged a brain capable of rational thought.

According to naturalists, the human brain—the only

reasoning organ we know of—is a product of the same random, accidental forces that produced the universe as a whole. It is nothing more than a chance cluster of molecules that came together by the random movements of nonrational forces.

Above, we demonstrated that when a thought can be shown to have an irrational cause—such as insanity in the case of the man who thought he was dead or hallucinogens in the case of the drug-addled writer—we know not to trust it. C. S. Lewis pointed out that this principle must apply to all thought in general: "We may in fact state it as a rule that *no thought is valid if it can be fully explained as the result of irrational causes.*"[2] If the universe is accidental, life on earth is accidental, evolution is accidental, and the human mind is accidental, then human thought is nothing more than the accidental movements of accidental atoms within an accidental brain. Why should we believe that thoughts produced by such a brain are capable of formulating a true account of reality? If all human thinking emanates from minds that evolved from a string of nonrational steps beginning with the nonrational cause that brought all matter into being, our thinking cannot be considered rational. To think reason could magically poof itself into existence in the course of the mind's nonrational evolutionary development resembles the medieval alchemists' futile hope that gold could be produced from lead.

Naturalists, of course, do trust in the rationality of thought despite their belief in a nonrationally produced mind. They use reason daily in their interactions with the phenomenal world, just as every sane person must. How do they reconcile these contradictory beliefs? Most of them probably give the question little or no thought. As we noted in chapter 3, we humans are capable of compartmentalizing our minds in ways that keep jarring contradictions from disturbing our tranquility. To ruthlessly examine deeply rooted assumptions that define our basis for belief is a painful process that most people assiduously avoid.

Some naturalists dip their toe into the postmodern pool and admit that they have no grounds for believing human thought to be valid. This does not bother them so long as reason produces practical results. They live by the premise that even if our thinking processes don't yield a true picture of reality, they work well enough to facilitate everyday living. But when naturalists adopt reason merely as a practical tool without defending its capacity to reveal truth, they lose all grounds for their assertion that naturalism is true. If they fail to endorse the validity of reason as a guide to truth, naturalism collapses for lack of rational support.

A naturalistic universe simply cannot supply from within itself validation for the rationality of human thought. A naturalistic universe and everything in it must be considered accidental, random, nonrational, and continually in a state of flux and unpredictability. In a naturalistic universe there is no bedrock, no solid footing to support human reason. Yet unless the lever of reason rests solidly on a firm and unmoving fulcrum, we cannot use human thought to pry the lid off truth or to uncover meaning for our lives. We contend that reason must have its origin in a rational mind that exists above the natural universe or our claim to be rational creatures is not credible.

Supernatural Intelligence as the Bedrock for Trusting Reason

We do not make the Enlightenment claim that reason can encompass all truth. We do, however, hold that all truth is rational and that adopting a belief that contradicts clear facts or plain reason is irrational. Contradictory claims cannot both be true.

We readily concede that some realities exist beyond the reach of reason, and we must not deny their existence simply because we lack the data to confirm them. It is not irrational to adopt a belief beyond our understanding as long as its known attributes do not contradict reason. For example, you may believe in the existence of black holes, extraterrestrial life, or the human spirit even though you can neither collect hard data on these concepts nor comprehend their mode of being. Despite the lack of hard evidence, such beliefs are not inherently irrational because nothing in our experience of reality contradicts their possible existence. Reason may be unable to entirely encompass or explain these phenomena, but neither can it credibly refute them.

While reason allows this kind of rational latitude, it will not allow us to believe in an outright contradiction. For example, we cannot believe in the simultaneous existence of both an immovable object and an irresistible force. If these two objects were to collide, one or the other—if not both—would be proved false. An immovable object and an irresistible force cannot exist simultaneously. They are by definition contradictory. If either exists, the other cannot, so to believe in both is irrational. We cannot synthesize opposites into a rational belief. We must choose one option as true and reject the other. Or where data is insufficient, we must simply suspend judgment.

If, as we have asserted, nonrational sources cannot produce an organ capable of reason, then our reasoning minds must necessarily be the product of a superior reasoning mind. Our ability to think rational thoughts that conform to reality could only have been infused into the human mind by a superior reasoning intelligence. This necessary inference traces reason to a solid, rational source outside the natural universe. With its source being superior to the natural universe, the rational mind is in a position to make judgments about the universe—about facts and truth and reality—that we can safely depend on as accurate.

Embracing God as the source of the rational universe solves the naturalistic dilemma concerning reason's validity. God as the creator of the rational mind gives reason bedrock support that guarantees its trustworthiness.

You can reject this conclusion, of course, just as you can reject belief in black holes, extraterrestrial life, and souls on the basis of insufficient empirical data. But belief in God does not qualify for rejection on the same basis. While the data on God is not of the sort that lends itself to scientific proof, nothing we know about him contradicts reason or our experience of reality. Though God is beyond the reach of empirical data, belief in him is not irrational. In fact, we contend that only through belief in God can you have any dependable sense that the universe is rational. If you reject God as reason's ultimate bedrock, you have nowhere else to turn. Deny God as the source of the human mind and you leave humanity adrift in a sea of irrationality. Your alternative to God is to live in a world of uncertainty about what is real and what is true.

It boils down to this: if you trust reason, you must believe in God. If you don't believe in God, you can't trust reason. Remove God as reason's absolute, and you pull the rug from under the belief that we are rational beings. When reason collapses, our certainty of any truth falls with it. To put it simply, either you believe in God or you cannot be sure there is anything to believe in at all. As we noted above, no one can live this way in the real world. Whether we realize it or choose not to think about it, we all live the essence of our lives in rational modes that imply the existence of a supernatural, rational being who is the source of humanity's capacity to reason.

Thinking Rationally in an Irrational Age

Though virtually everyone believes in the validity of reason when applied to practical matters, we live in an age when reason seems rarely applied to values. We probably see this most in the accusations slung about in politics, news media, and social media: "The Black candidate lost because the voters are racists." "The woman wasn't hired because the company is sexist." "The house voted against the bill because it would help the opposing party."

Accusations such as these are almost always based on emotion rather than reason. The accusers give no credence to the possibility that the denounced act may have had a rational cause. The white candidate may have better reflected the voters' politics. The woman simply may not have been qualified for the position. The bill may have been voted down on its own merits.

In his book *Amusing Ourselves to Death*, Neil Postman points to a factor that may explain why objective thinking has slipped dramatically in the secular age. He claims that our immersion in entertainment media has diluted our capacity to reason. Television and movies, for example, keep our minds in a passive mode and require no active response. Reading, on the other hand, requires interaction and mental analysis, which exercise the brain's rational capacities. The increase of exposure to these passive entertainment media and the decline of reading may explain this drop in rational thinking so clearly exhibited in news and social media today. According to Postman, the more entertained we are, the less we are able to understand and respond to the complex challenges of our day.[3]

Human nature makes it easy for any of us to skew our thinking by basing conclusions on irrational premises. When reason points away from the results we prefer, it's easy to reach for an irrational premise to justify our desires. We may say we disbelieve in God because we find the evidence unconvincing, when the real reason—likely hidden even to ourselves—is that admitting God's existence would call for changing our lifestyle, giving up practices hard to relinquish, enduring the scorn of peers, or getting out of step with current societal norms.

It's also hard to be objective when our personal desires or status or reputation are threatened. Naturalists who have taken pride in their lifetime defense of atheism may find it a nearly insurmountable difficulty to admit they have been wrong.

Whether or not these difficulties apply to you, when it comes to belief in God, the stakes are so terribly high that we urge you to examine your reasons for disbelief as closely, honestly, objectively, and relentlessly as you can.

We will close this chapter by giving you one of our most elemental reasons for believing in God. Even though you may have doubts about his existence, we are pretty sure that you believe in the existence of a supernatural realm of some kind. In fact, the existence of such a realm is unquestionable. To understand why this is so, let's look at the only three alternatives available to explain the existence of anything at all:

Option 1: Everything that exists has always existed.

Option 2: Everything came into existence on its own out of nothing, with no external cause.

Option 3: Everything was created by a self-existent, intelligent being.

These are the only possible options to explain existence, and all three are by nature impossible. That is, there is no possible natural explanation for the existence of anything at all. Every possible explanation for existence defies nature because for it to occur according to the laws of nature is impossible.

Option 1 is impossible because nothing can by nature exist always. Nature demands that everything that exists must have a beginning. For anything to exist eternally means existence had no beginning, which takes us outside the realm of what nature allows and pushes us into supernaturalism.

Option 2 defies nature because it is impossible for the existence of anything to emerge naturally out of nothing. The uncaused emergence of matter and energy would put beginnings into the realm of the supernatural.

Option 3 is impossible for the same reason Option 1 is impossible. It demands the presence of a self-existent, all-powerful being, and nothing in nature can be self-existent. For any being to exist eternally takes us outside the realm of nature and puts beginnings into the realm of the supernatural.

Yet, one of these options must be true, because things do exist. This fact inevitably thrusts the answer to origins into a realm outside nature, which is by definition a supernatural realm. Put simply, the existence of anything at all forces us to accept the presence of a realm or a being that is outside what we know as nature. Once we accept the undeniability of a supernatural realm—which the very fact of existence forces us to do—we have no rationale for excluding the possibility of God.

We are convinced that of the three explanations for existence, the third is the most rational. Yes, we realize that to posit God as the originator of the universe merely shoves the mystery of origins back a step. How did God come into being? How could he exist always? Eternal existence is impossible by the laws of nature, but given the necessity of choosing from among options that reason cannot encompass, God seems to offer the most rational explanation. He explains the existence not only of matter and energy but also of natural law, life, conscious thought, and reason. He puts the reality we experience on solid footing, whereas naturalism with its premise of random, nonrational origins does not.

We fully realize that the conclusions we propose here are antipathetic to the secularism of the day, but we urge you not to dismiss them out of hand. The search for truth is neither a trivial pursuit nor a mere intellectual exercise. It is of vital importance because of what is riding on the outcome, which is nothing less than your eternal destiny. If we find that absolute truth exists, many other realities that modern and postmodern secularists might prefer to shut out may exist as well. If God exists as creator, his claims of truth are enormously important realities that we must come to grips with. We must doggedly pursue the answers to these questions or face the possibility of immeasurable consequences. Reason is necessary as a guide in that search. That is why the validity of reason is a question of such vital importance.

QUESTIONS FOR THOUGHT AND DISCUSSION

1. Can experience, worldviews, and environment undermine reason's dependability? Why or why not?

2. Why can't reason validate its own dependability?

3. How can we know that reason is dependable?

4. Could random natural forces have produced reason? Explain.

5. If God is not the source of reason, can reason validate truth? Explain why or why not.

6. Why does reason need a bedrock absolute outside nature to be valid?

7. What are the only three available options to account for all existence? What is your reaction to the idea that all three of these point to the existence of a realm outside of nature?

5

THE MYSTIFYING MYSTERY OF MORALITY

Is our concept of right and wrong absolute or obsolete?

At lunch Mark and a coworker decided to try out a new restaurant that had just opened a few blocks from the office. As Mark pulled into the parking lot, he spotted a space just vacated right next to the door. "Aha, I'm in luck," he said as he turned into the lane and drove toward the slot. He had begun to turn into it when a young woman in a little Honda zoomed toward him from the opposite direction. As he slammed on his brakes to avoid a collision, she whipped into his parking space.

"Of all the nerve!" Mark cried. "Did you ever see anything so rude? She knew good and well I was about to pull in there." He was still seething as he and his friend entered the restaurant. He saw the offending woman being seated and seriously considered confronting her.

"Come on, Mark, just let it go," said his friend. But it took a while for Mark to calm down.

Why was Mark so upset? At issue was nothing more than a parking space. Plenty of other spaces were available, and the inconvenience of walking a little farther was not exactly on par with trekking ten miles through the Sahara. It wasn't as if Mark had been cheated out of his inheritance or placed in jeopardy of losing life or health. Furthermore, no laws or statutes define rights to a public parking space. It's not one of the Ten Commandments.

Yet these tirades over behavior not prescribed by official rules or law tell us something. They demonstrate that everyone possesses an innate sense of right and wrong. We all believe we ought to be treated fairly and courteously. We assume that those around us know innately what right behavior is and should act accordingly.

Some people deny that we possess this innate understanding, and we all occasionally act as if we didn't. Yet despite these sporadic departures, our responses to the offending behavior of others show clearly that we have an inborn sense of right and wrong. We would not yell at rude drivers unless we believed rude driving to be wrong. It makes no sense to express anger at bad behavior unless we recognize a commonly accepted standard for good behavior. In fact, before you can dispute anything with another person, the two of you must agree on one thing: a standard that defines right and wrong. Disputants must share a common standard that defines right before either can expect to convince the other that the standard has been violated.

These drivers' tirades over simple personal offenses not codified by law indicate on a microcosmic level what Christianity and other religions have long held to be an overarching universal truth: built into each of us is an all-encompassing moral standard that is absolute, authoritative, unchangeable, and universally applicable. With the advent of secularism, however, this claim has come under fire. Traditional morality is now being challenged as an obstacle to freedom and human flourishing, and its claim to authority has been dismissed as spurious and unprovable. In this chapter we will address these challenges.

The Universal Nature of Morality

Before the modern era of Western secularism, virtually everyone took morality for granted. Even today, with traditional morality under attack, we still find a sense of morality in every society around the world, from the most primitive to the most advanced. We find it not only in all present cultures but also in the records of all past cultures. The moral codes of all these societies are surprisingly similar no matter how widely separated by time, geography, development, or religion.

The morality defined in the Jewish Ten Commandments, the ancient Babylonian Code of Hammurabi, the Chinese

Tao Te Ching, and the Christian New Testament differ in detail and emphasis but not in essence. Some societies allow individuals to kill to avenge a wrong, while others reserve penal execution as the prerogative of the state. Some allow polygamy while others maintain monogamy. Property rights vary from culture to culture. In ancient Israel, land titles reverted to the original owner families every fifty years.

Yet despite these and other variations, all societies have had rules that people cannot kill others at will or engage in sex with just anyone or take what another owns. All have laws protecting human life; all have rules governing marriage and family relationships; all condemn stealing; all encourage doing good to others.

Of course, every society has within it people who resist the imposition of morality on their behavior. When a sufficient number of these gain power, significant deviations from the universal moral sense can occur. We saw it in Nazi Germany and in the killing of female infants in some Asian countries. Usually these aberrations are short-lived, as outrage leads those within or outside the society to rise up and stop the aberrant behavior. Yet despite these occasional variations and distortions, the same basic sense of morality appears wherever humans congregate. It's as if many orchestras are playing the same symphony but adapting the harmonics to fit their own instruments.

How can we explain a moral code that is so consistently present in all societies? How do we explain a sense of morality that gives every sane person on the planet a common and innate sense of right and wrong? Why should such a moral sense exist at all? Let's look first at three of the most common naturalistic explanations.

The Invention Theory of Morality

The invention theory explains morality as a set of rules for self-preservation that humans have devised through trial and error over time. The theory asserts that nothing about these rules is absolute. They were not handed down by some mountaintop god but grew out of humanity's own common sense and practical thinking. The driving purpose behind moral behavior is not conformity to some overarching, supernatural truth, but simple survival. What we call morality is merely a set of guidelines that humans have found to work when huddled together for mutual protection in hostile environments. Behavior that helps or strengthens society is encouraged and called right. Behavior that hurts or weakens it is prohibited and called wrong.

A major flaw lies hidden within the invention theory. Whenever people try to determine right for themselves, they always start by assuming that some underlying principle is already intrinsically right. As we observed in chapter 2, when people claim that morality is simply humankind's invention to preserve society, they tacitly assume that *society ought to be preserved*. This axiomatic assumption is the bedrock on which their morality rests. They may deny that any absolute authority for morality exists, but the moment they make any kind of foundational moral claim—which is what the proposition that society ought to be preserved is—they plant their feet on a moral absolute. They cannot do otherwise because for any assumption to be held valid, it must have the support of a bedrock absolute. Naturalists may lock the door against absolutes of any kind, but the moment they claim any action to be intrinsically right or wrong, some kind of absolute has sneaked in through the window.

How can anyone dispute the proposition that society ought to be preserved? It seems too obvious to question. But is it? It can be neither proved nor supported by reason. From the naturalists' point of view, it can be worse than unreasonable; it can be intrusive and unfairly demanding. Time allots to each of us only a few precious years on earth before we exit human society through the ever-gaping portal of death. Why should we care if civilization survives past our own funeral? Why should we expend precious time and energy to advance the survival of others who live after us when we have no stake in their future?

Yet despite the lack of a rationale for altruism, naturalists the world over make sacrifices for the good of society. They stop to help stranded motorists. They donate to feed starving children. They give blood, and they volunteer in the wake of natural disasters. They become police officers, firefighters, nurses, soldiers. Agnostic Bill Gates, who has been quoted as saying, "I don't know if there's a god or not,"[1] has donated billions of dollars to charities.

Why do they do it? Why do unbelievers who think

existence ends with death choose to devote time, energy, and money to looking out for others? Many would reply that it's simply the right, unselfish, and noble thing to do. They are, no doubt, speaking sincerely because they feel the values of rightness, unselfishness, and nobility embedded in their hearts. But those feelings are inconsistent with their denial of God. Terms like unselfishness, sacrifice, and concern for others are intrusions on the naturalist's short and precious life. If there is no God to prescribe such unselfish behavior and no hope of eternal reward for making the sacrifice, the only approach that makes sense for naturalists is to pack into every precious moment all the pleasure and gratification they can grab. Let society take care of its own future.

Despite what makes sense, theists and naturalists alike are saddled with the notion that there are certain things all humans *ought* to do. We ought to give aid to those in need. We ought to defend children against abuse. We ought to be honest and truthful. No one, whether naturalist or theist, can break free from the tug of these oughts. They grip us like gravity. When we look beneath these oughts, we find them rooted in the assumed absolute moral principle that society ought to be preserved. That idea should mean nothing to naturalists, yet they can't get rid of it. It's like trying to throw away a boomerang—it keeps coming back. The concept is firmly entrenched within the mind of every sane human, yet human reason cannot defend it. It defies rational explanation in a naturalistic universe.

Here is the dilemma of naturalists: since they cannot

prove by reason that society ought to be preserved, they must choose between two alternatives:

1. Accept the idea as an absolute imperative.
2. Reject it as an outrageous demand in a godless universe where self is accountable to no one.

If they accept it as an absolute, they lose their rationale for being naturalists. Such a counterintuitive moral concept can have force only if it has roots in an absolute god to whom we are responsible. If naturalists reject God as the authority behind this moral principle, they must dismiss the tug of their hearts toward duty to others as an illusion. Of course, even if they dismiss it, they still may choose to give in to it—not because they think it is an absolute imperative but merely because doing right by others makes them feel good or placates their conscience.

If the preservation of society is an absolute truth from God, then the universal moral law has force. If, on the other hand, the preservation of society is merely a human concept, then the moral laws invented to support it are grossly unfair because they contradict the rights of the individual to live his short life solely for his own benefit.

In a world without God, it would be meaningless for Mark to express outrage at the young woman who stole his parking place. She was just doing what benefited her at the moment. What more should we expect from an evolution-produced machine? Unless God is the authority behind morality, we cannot expect anyone to drive or live according to any standard society invents. We cannot blame people for dedicating their lives to their own pleasure. Without a transcendent God as bedrock, we have no standard to justify the assertion that doing good to others is any better than ignoring the needs of others and doing good only for ourselves. If there is no God, there can be no such thing as true and absolute right. All rules are mere opinion, and none has authority. If there is no God to give humankind a hope for life after death, we can ignore any notions of rightness that self-appointed moralists shove at us, and we can get on with the business of pleasing ourselves. As Russian novelist Fyodor Dostoyevsky wrote in *The Brothers Karamazov*, "If there is no immortality of the soul, there can be no virtue and therefore everything is permissible."[2]

Let us be up front and admit it: a world in which everything is permissible has a certain surface appeal. All of us harbor within ourselves an impulse to kick aside the rules, flex our freedom, ignore the restrictions of moral law, and do just what we please. But it won't work. When we remove the restrictions of moral law, we also remove its protections. Without law we cannot expect to be treated fairly or safely because society's capacity to protect life and property evaporates. Stable relationships become impossible. Marriages disintegrate. Families fall apart. Honesty evaporates. Murder, rape, rioting, and theft become rampant. Order decays into anarchy, and communal life takes on the character of a lawless jungle. Theologian/philosopher William Lane Craig writes:

One Rabbi who was imprisoned at Auschwitz said
that it was as though all the Ten Commandments
had been reversed: thou shalt kill, thou shalt lie, thou
shalt steal. Mankind has never seen such a hell. And
yet, in a real sense, if naturalism is true, our world is
Auschwitz. There is no good and evil, no right and
wrong. Objective moral values do not exist.[3]

Whether God exists is not merely a theoretical question
with no practical bearing on our everyday lives. As belief in
God wanes, moral authority loses force, and the underpin-
nings of society begin to crumble.

The Social Contract Theory of Morality

The social contract theory can be expressed like this: "We
all want freedom to live our own lives in our own way. We
need moral laws to limit the potentially intrusive behavior
of others so we can get on with the business of doing our
own thing. Since we deny the existence of a transcendent
moral lawgiver, we adhere to mutually accepted moral rules
as a social contract among the individuals within society. By
consensus, we agree to follow these rules, each giving up a
little freedom so that all can enjoy a reasonable measure of
freedom." Governments manage the social contract, express-
ing the moral will of society by enacting and enforcing laws
that define standards for behavior.

The social contract theory contains two flaws, both deadly.

First, if moral rules carry no more authority than majority consensus, the individual is no longer impelled to obey them when they conflict with personal desires.

This is similar to the flaw that dooms the invention theory. People may honor the social contract as long as they find it convenient or because it helps them avoid punishment or even because they realize the value of its protections. But those who believe morality to be without absolute authority will not take obedience seriously when it conflicts with their deepest desires. They will obey only when it doesn't interfere with their own ends or when the risk of disobedience is too great.

If there is no God, this indifferent, self-referential approach to law is perfectly reasonable—but utterly fatal. The refusal to recognize God as the absolute authority behind right and wrong will eventually cause a society to destroy itself. People will increasingly chip away at the restrictions of law to gain more and more freedom to follow their urges. Governments, following the will of their constituents, will gradually loosen the restrictions. As law relaxes its restraint on individual urges, altruism will erode, and individualism will increase to the point that allegiance to society as a whole evaporates. People will become focused largely on themselves—their own rights, wants, and pleasures. Deprived of the lifeblood of a true and absolute morality, motivation to sacrifice personal satisfaction for duty to others will shrivel and die.

The second flaw in the social contract theory is that a disintegrating society adrift with no moral anchor will fall under the control of tyrannical leaders driven by a lust for power to control others.

This second fatal flaw of the social contract theory rears its menacing head in response to the first. When society begins to fragment into self-centered individualism, the population becomes vulnerable to the tyranny of what philosopher Friedrich Nietzsche called "the will to power." With no overarching guide to right and wrong, these autocratic controllers will ignore the social contract and impose their own will upon the people they govern. The basis for morality becomes "might makes right," and right is defined as whatever those in power want it to be.

When leaders displace morality with sheer power, the results are hideous. Vladimir Lenin became leader of Russia after the 1917 Bolshevik Revolution. He resorted to mass executions and terror to solidify his rule, using, as he himself put it, "unrestricted power based on force, not law."[4] Lenin and his successor, Joseph Stalin, eliminated opposition by stripping their subjects of property, freedom, dignity, justice, and life. They executed millions of their own countrymen.

When morality is determined by consensus, it inevitably results in the strong victimizing the weak. Today we see secularists applauding as government grants its constituents greater sexual license and overrides the rights of those who adhere to traditional morality. History shows, however, that the beneficiaries of evolving moral laws today often become its victims tomorrow. With no firm and authoritative moral code, no one is safe from the next wave of political fashion, which will be determined by those who have accumulated the most power.

America's Founding Fathers understood that the law governing a nation should be more than a mere social contract. The Declaration of Independence explicitly recognized God as the authority behind law when it proposed severing the American colonies from England and assuming "the separate and equal station to which the Laws of Nature and of Nature's God entitle them." Now Nature's God is being pushed aside as the absolute behind moral law. A growing number of Americans believe the government, not God, is the source of law, and the government is happily accepting this transferred authority. Those in power seem determined to accede to constituents bent on overriding any moral principle that restricts the unlimited satisfaction of all urges.

The movers and shakers of our secular age don't seem to realize that the only way a people's freedom can be preserved is to recognize an unchangeable morality that equally constrains both the rulers and the ruled. Remove this overarching protection and good becomes whatever society's rulers decide it should be. The ruling class will assume the license to decide what is good for the rest. Only by subjecting both the rulers and the ruled to an objective moral standard above nature and immune to manipulation can tyranny be averted.

The secular idea of progress currently being thrust upon us by those in power includes the claim that the future will be better than the past if we simply remove restrictions of morality. This claim is a myth. History shows clearly that when the powers governing nations dispose of the universal moral code, they sign their own death warrant. Their regimes always implode upon themselves. The need to hide this fact is one of the reasons today's progressives are committed to rewriting American history. The moral principles that guided the US for most of its two centuries of success must be obliterated if the progressive agenda is to gain traction. The fact that no nation has ever survived the undermining of the universal moral code must be concealed.

A primary reason conservative Christian churches are currently under fire is that they refuse to "move with the times" and accede to the secularists' demand for changes to the universal moral code. In refusing to adjust to modern and postmodern morality, the church is accused of impeding human progress. Think it through and you will see that this is an irrational accusation. We can have progress only if we recognize the existence of a fixed, unmoving end point. A football team can progress toward a touchdown only if the goal line remains fixed. Remove that line or allow it to flex and no progress is possible. We can progress toward a better society only if we strive to conform to a fixed, overarching standard for what a good society is—and that is exactly what objective morality gives us.

Society cannot survive a moral code based on nothing more than a social contract. When we try to determine right by consensus, we are guided solely by our immediate and changing desires. We lack the wisdom to see the long-term result of our choices, which is why the universal moral code does not cater to our immediate urges. Those urges may lead us to covet our neighbor's car or home or spouse—but that moral code says we can't have them. We may think a little white lie will enhance our reputation, but that old morality says we can't tell it. Objective morality warns us that our immoral urges can obstruct our long-term good by drawing us like baited bugs into traps of addiction, damaged relationships, and ruined character.

The Instinct Theory of Morality

The third naturalistic explanation for morality is the instinct theory. This theory tells us that nature embedded a concept of right and wrong within humanity to ensure cooperation and fair play, which are necessary for survival. The evolutionary process genetically programmed us with moral instincts that spur us toward self-preserving behavior. When we behave morally, we are merely obeying an instinct implanted by nature.

The basic flaw in the instinct theory is this: before we can obey nature, we must ask which nature we should obey.

Nature often confronts us with conflicting urges. We commonly feel urges to satisfy our personal desires, achieve our ambitions, pursue pleasure, and gratify self. In opposition to these natural urges, however, we can also feel moved to help a stranded motorist, patiently soothe a screaming infant, sit up all night with a sick friend, or even sacrifice our life for another person.

Often a pair of these contradicting urges will confront us simultaneously, forcing us to decide between them. We've all seen this conflict pictured humorously as a person harassed by a little angel perched on one shoulder and a little demon on the other. When a driver sees a stranded motorist beside the highway, the angel urges him, "Pull over, and offer assistance. It's the right thing to do. Wouldn't you want someone to do the same for you?" From the other shoulder comes the voice of the demon: "Don't stop. You'll be late for your appointment. You'll get your new slacks dirty. You might even get mugged."

No doubt you yourself have had to choose between such competing urges as a daily occurrence. *Shall I be patient with my obstinate teenager or blow my stack again? Shall I help my spouse with the dishes or watch my favorite TV program? Shall I cut my employee some slack for being late or dock his pay?* The options can be more serious: *Shall I race to the cellar as the tornado approaches or run to my neighbor's yard to rescue her child playing in the sandbox?*

Few would disagree about the right choices in the examples above. We all admire people who put the needs of others ahead of their own, and we scorn those who put themselves first. But if all our urges come from nature, isn't it strange that they so often conflict with each other? Isn't it even more strange that we applaud one option and condemn the other? By what standard do we make such a judgment? It can't be by any standard nature provides because that would have nature contradicting itself. The call to make a right decision when faced with two competing urges implies the presence of a standard that exists above both—a standard completely independent of nature. If all urges come from nature, the standard by which we judge between them must necessarily be rooted in a source outside nature.

But wait. Can we be sure that both of these conflicting urges come from nature? When we examine the motivation to save a neighbor's child from a tornado, can we truly say that there is anything natural about it? We know the urge to head straight for the cellar to save oneself comes from nature; self-preservation is a recognized natural instinct. But what is natural about a person deliberately risking his life to perform a dangerous, heroic act that cannot possibly benefit him? It's clear that the impulse to sacrifice oneself for another person's child cannot come from nature. Personal sacrifice for the sake of others runs against the natural urge of self-preservation. Yet theists and naturalists alike applaud it as the highest of virtues.

We can see that the concept of morality as an instinct implanted by nature has one big, obvious problem. *If it comes from nature, why isn't it natural?* Why does morality so often prod us to act in opposition to other urges we clearly recognize as natural? We understand our urges to go with the flow, to give in to self-serving desires, to protect ourselves at all costs, to avoid risks that offer no benefit. But then along come those inexplicable urges issuing from that meddlesome mystery we call conscience, butting in uninvited and spoiling our party. Our conscience is the voice of morality, telling us not to do that thing we really want to do, not because refraining will make us better off—indeed, it often seems to make us worse off, at least immediately—but simply because it isn't right. You want to keep the twenty-dollar bill the cashier accidentally gave you in change, but that persistent voice, which you wish would hush up and go away, prods you to give it back. You want to copy the test paper you can so easily see on your classmate's desk, but that irksome voice tells you to keep your eyes to yourself. You want to omit a cash receipt from your tax return, but that exasperating voice urges you to report it. Morality is not natural. It is too much at odds with our natural desires to share kinship with them. Morality is obviously an intruder from somewhere outside nature.

The True Meaning of Morality

All the naturalistic explanations for morality overlook the same essential difficulty: morality simply does not align well with human nature. The invention and social contract theories don't work because, had humankind invented the rules of right and wrong, they would be more compatible with natural human impulses. If you were inventing a new language, you would devise words your tongue could form easily and naturally. Conforming to morality, however, is like trying to speak a language from another galaxy. Morality asks us to perform in ways that are neither easy nor natural, the opposite of what we would expect of a human invention.

The instinct theory presents the same basic problem. If

morality is an instinct that evolved with the human race, right behavior should be as natural for us as for salmon to swim upstream to spawn or for geese to fly south for the winter. We would always do the right thing without even thinking about it. But doing the right thing is seldom natural or easy. We find ourselves in continual conflict with our sense of right and wrong, yet we can't get rid of it. It's like a catchy tune we keep humming long after we're sick of hearing it.

Who wrote that tune? If morality did not come from ourselves or from nature, where did it come from? Ethicist Richard Taylor tells us there is only one rational option:

> Without God as the source, any rational explanation for morality collapses. The modern age, more or less repudiating the idea of a divine lawgiver, has nevertheless tried to retain the ideas of moral right and wrong, not noticing that, in casting God aside, they have also abolished the conditions of meaningfulness for moral right and wrong as well.[5]

Dr. Taylor is right. Either God is the source of morality, or morality has no rational explanation. It is an inexplicable illusion. Of those two options, it is utterly rational to accept the idea that God is the author of morality and the authority who stands behind it. He wired us with that embedded moral sense that all sane humans feel operating within themselves.

Why would God burden us with a morality that so rudely intrudes on our wants and urges? The short answer, as we noted above, is to keep our natural urges from plunging us into disaster. To link moral license with societal collapse may seem an alarmist overstatement—but is it? We cannot deny that twenty-first-century America is undergoing societal convulsions. Though we may dispute the causes, we can see ominous shadows gathering as America's two centuries of social cohesion fragment into self-focused individualism. Distrust is smoldering between races, economic classes, political parties, religions, and sexes. People are beginning to withdraw into themselves, closing off from meaningful face-to-face relationships and retreating into the electronic world of Internet, smartphones, virtual reality, and social media.

This growing trend toward isolated individualism allows distrust to fester into hate, which today is spewed across the Internet in poisonous tweets and hashtags. We now perceive culture as being largely divided into bullies and victims. No one feels safe. We see ourselves as potential victims of people to whom the concept of objective values is utterly foreign.

Is it possible that our banishment of God has anything to do with this societal deterioration? There is considerable logic to the idea. As the smog of secularism chokes out belief in God, the overarching canopy of protective morality disappears. Unless this gathering cloud of corrosive acid is lifted, we can expect the darkness to deepen as relationships continue to erode.

We can forestall societal collapse by regrouping under the umbrella of objective morality. By recovering the universal moral code, we can reverse our fragmentation, rebuild trust,

and restore relationships. Authentic morality provides guidelines for interpersonal conduct and makes stable relationships possible. The absolutes of right and wrong provide a
template to guide us in loving our families and our neighbors and in treating others fairly. Bottom line: morality is all
about how to love effectively, and love banishes mistrust and
self-centeredness.

Why is it right to stop and help stranded motorists but
wrong to veer over and run them down? The moral code tells
us that helping is right because moral principles come from
God and reflect his nature. His nature is love, and rendering
help is an act of love. This loving helpfulness that morality
encourages creates a healthy society. The objective standard
underscoring morality is the timeless Golden Rule, which
predates Christianity and reaches back into the ancient
world: "Do for others as you wish them to do for you."

Why do you feel a stab of conscience when you lie to
your spouse, parent, child, or boss? It is because deceit and
distrust erode relationships, while honesty and truthfulness bond people together with trust. Truthfulness is loving
because it protects you from the pain of damaged relationships that results from duplicity. The same is true for all the
other "oughts" and "ought nots" that make up authentic
morality.

Morality is like the manual for maintaining your automo-
bile. It tells you how the human organism should be run, gives
guidance for identifying malfunctions, and provides instructions for repair. When we understand the benefits of morality,

its irritations become easier to bear. God desires that we live not in lonely isolation, but in joyful, satisfying relationships. Morality flows to us from his own nature as our guide to maintaining and nurturing those relationships.

QUESTIONS FOR THOUGHT AND DISCUSSION

1. How can we explain the similarity of morality in all societies in all places at all times?

2. Why isn't it possible that morality is humanity's invention for preserving society?

3. What is the flaw in thinking morality is a social contract reflecting the consensus of society?

4. How do we know that morality is not merely instinctual or natural?

5. Why is it illogical for naturalists to submit to any imposed code of morality?

6. Explain Dostoyevsky's statement, "If there is no immortality of the soul, there can be no virtue and therefore everything is permissible."

7. What does morality mean to you personally and to your relationships?

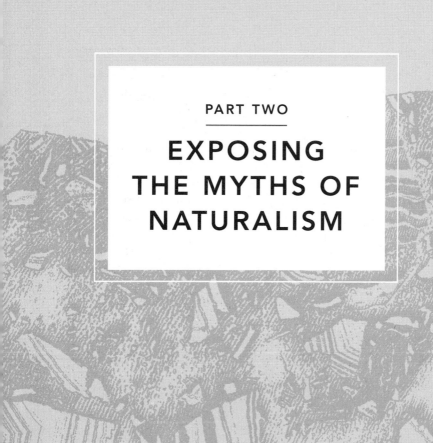

PART TWO

EXPOSING
THE MYTHS OF
NATURALISM

THE MIND-BENDING
MYSTERY OF ORIGINS

The existence of anything seems impossible,
yet here we are.

One day a little girl asked her mother the inevitable question that all parents dread: "Mommy, where did I come from?" This mother had known the question would come sooner or later, so she was well-prepared. She took her daughter to the den, pulled from the shelf a basic book on human reproduction, along with several charts and diagrams she had accumulated, and spent the next hour explaining all the processes involved in making human babies.

When she finished, she said to her daughter, "So, that is where you came from. Have I answered your question?"

"Well, yes, I guess so," replied the little girl. "My friend Shirley said she came from Chicago, so I just wondered where I came from."

Sooner or later, we all begin to ask questions about our

origins. As young children we want to know where we came from—not where we were born, but how we came into existence as a person. As we grow older, our questions about origins grow larger, and we want to know how everything that exists came into being.

Naturalistic scientists have developed three theories to explain the origins of everything. The first explains the origin of the universe, the second explains the origin of life, and the third explains the origin of all the species of plants and animals living on the earth today. In this chapter we will address the first two of these theories—the origin of the universe and the origin of life. We will reserve discussion of the origin of the species for the following chapter.

How Did the Universe Come to Be?

The dominant naturalistic theory of origins proposes that approximately 13.7 billion years ago, nothing at all existed except for what physicists call a "singularity." This was a zone of gravitational pressure so intense that it squeezed finite matter into an infinitely hot mass of infinite density. Then that microscopic concentration of matter underwent a sudden expansion. In rapid succession, protons and neutrons formed, nucleosynthesis occurred, and these subatomic particles formed the nuclei of the first atoms. About 300 to 500 million years later, the first stars and galaxies came into being as these atoms began to coalesce. The universe continued to expand, cool, and organize into specific configurations until it reached its present size, form, and temperature. And, according to the theory, it continues to expand.

This explanation for the origin of the universe was initially proposed by Belgian mathematician Georges Lemaître in 1931. He called it the "hypothesis of the primeval atom." Today it is the theory most commonly accepted by naturalists (and some theists) and is popularly known as the *big bang theory*. The big bang, however, is not the only model explaining the existence of the universe. Many respected physicists hold to other models, such as the *static space-time paradigm*—the idea that the universe has always existed and is unchanging in its size—but they remain in the minority. The 2019 Nobel Prize–winning physicist James Peebles rejects the big bang theory for simple lack of evidence. He says, "It's very unfortunate that one thinks of the beginning whereas in fact, we have no good theory of such a thing as the beginning." He adds, "We don't have a strong test of what happened earlier in time. We have theories, but not tested."[1]

While the big bang theory could possibly explain several observable phenomena in the universe, it stops short of explaining the universe's ultimate origin. It does not explain the origin of that primal singularity (the ultradense concentration of matter), the energy that propelled the expansion, the force that triggered it, or the laws by which the scattering atoms eventually assembled themselves into various orderly forms. Where those masses and forces came from and why they appeared remains unsolved. One scientific website describes the big bang theory as several hundred billion stars "in a galaxy soaring through the cosmos, all of which is inside of an expanding universe that began as an infinitesimal singularity which appeared out of nowhere for reasons unknown."[2] Before we can have an adequate and coherent explanation of origins, that singularity's appearance "out of nowhere" and those "reasons unknown" for its appearance need to be accounted for.

Some physicists, such as the late Stephen Hawking and Leonard Mlodinow, recognized the need for a naturalistic explanation for the existence of that original singularity. In their book *The Grand Design*, they proposed a theory that the universe could have emerged from nothing. They hypothesized that "because there is a law such as gravity, the universe can and will create itself from nothing. . . . Spontaneous creation is the reason there is something rather than nothing, why the universe exists, why we exist. It is not necessary to invoke God to light the blue touch paper and set the universe going."[3]

The problem with this explanation is immediately obvious. The presence of "a law such as gravity" admits to a force and a governing law that preexist and initiate this creation from "nothing." We cannot escape the logic that nothing can come from nothing. The source of these prematter forces needs to be explained or Hawking and Mlodinow have no real theory of ultimate origins.

Furthermore, the theory is light years away from being settled science. A 2019 article in the online Quanta Magazine says, "A recent challenge to Stephen Hawking's biggest idea—about how the universe might have come from nothing—has cosmologists choosing sides." The article reports serious rebuttals to Hawking by physicists Neil Turok, Job Feldbrugge, and Jean-Luc Lehners. Other scientists soon joined the discussion, and the debate continues.[4]

Yet despite the controversy over theories, naturalistic scientists continue to assume that not only the material forms in the universe, but also the laws that enable atoms to coalesce into molecules, cells, and complex organisms were produced by random, undirected nature. These assumptions run counter to a firmly established, inviolable natural law: chaos, left to itself, never produces order. Never. The well-known second law of thermodynamics tells us that "in a closed system, no processes will tend to occur that increase the net organization (or decrease the net entropy) of the system. Thus, the universe taken as a whole is steadily moving toward a state of complete randomness."[5] To put it simply, nature moves order toward chaos, not vice versa. This means that if the naturalistic explanation for the universe is correct, we must believe that in bringing everything into existence, nature has violated its own inviolable law. It has brought extremely intricate order out of undirected chaos.

Naturalism postulates *time* as the element that enables order to emerge from chaos. Given enough time—hundreds of millions of years—random atoms flying through space began to form stars, planets, and galaxies. All this occurred without direction or purpose. Time alone was the magician.

An illustration used to demonstrate how time can produce

order is known as the *infinite monkey theorem*. The theorem says that if a monkey with a computer were given an infinite span of time, it would by randomly striking the keyboard eventually produce all the works of Shakespeare.

As we are sure you would agree, reason refutes this theorem easily. Given all eternity, a typing monkey would never produce even the first line of dialogue from *Macbeth*, which contains seventy-three characters including spaces, complicated by italics, capitals, and punctuation: "*First Witch*: When shall we three meet again? In thunder, lightning, or in rain?" The order of letters, spaces, and punctuation is too specific for exact duplication of more than a few letters to occur from random keyboarding. No doubt a correctly spelled word or even a correctly placed combination of a few words might occur occasionally. But these would always be interspersed with random and meaningless letters, spaces, and punctuation that would prevent a meaningful sequence of significant length from ever appearing. Time would not increase the odds, for randomness would eternally rule every segment of the sequence.

The only way the monkey could reproduce any work of literature would be to have an intelligent being monitor its output. Whenever the monkey duplicated a short, intelligible word sequence, the monitor would save it and add it to others produced throughout eons of time until the monkey finally produced all the needed words or phrases, which the monitor would arrange in the required sequence. Then voilà! One could claim that the monkey had typed Shakespeare's entire corpus. The resulting order, however, would not have been produced by random mindlessness. It would have been imposed by an intelligent organizer.

There is no certified, recognized, or observable law of nature that will account for order emerging out of mindless chaos. In fact, order emerging from chaos contradicts the long-known and inviolable law of entropy. As we noted above, entropy says (in a nutshell) that everything is running down. Left to itself, nature scatters, erodes, breaks down, and wears out. Life always plays out into death; the organic decays into the inorganic. Energy is consumed and resources are depleted, never to be fully replaced in the cycle of nature. Planets slow infinitesimally with each orbit. Stars burn out and disintegrate. The reality we consistently observe is a universe irrevocably running down.

Yet naturalism asks us to believe in exceptions to the law of entropy—that since its inception, the universe has been winding itself up. It has become increasingly orderly, organized, and efficient. The problem with this claim is that no evidence of such upward progress exists, and no known scientific principle can account for it. In fact, it flagrantly violates consistent observation, experience, and established laws of physics. It's easy to become so impressed and overwhelmed by the technical explanations of details supporting naturalistic theories of origins that we forget the inevitable irrationality that lies beneath them. Something can never come naturally from nothing. To have a rational theory of origins, this inviolable principle must be consistently applied to matter, energy, and life.

How Did Life Arise on Earth?

The naturalistic explanation for the origin of life is expressed in a theory known as *abiogenesis*. Abiogenesis asserts that life on earth arose from nonliving organic compounds. According to the theory, a delicately balanced combination of randomly assembled chemicals fused under ideal conditions to form simple organic cells. An electrical current passed through the cells, giving them not only life but also the immediate ability to replicate themselves through mitosis (cell division). Here is a simplified summary of more complex explanations of abiogenesis found on scientific websites:

> The *modern hypothesis of abiogenesis* holds that the primitive life on Earth originated from lifeless matter and it took millions of years to transpire. This theory is the widely-accepted premise on the *origin of life*. . . . How abiogenesis occurred is still a mystery. It probably incorporated various processes such as self-replication, self-assembly, autocatalysis, and cell membrane formation. . . . It is hypothesized that . . . life emerging from the non-living came about as a gradual process that took millions of years. And, this transformation of non-living matter into *living* entity has not been repeated since then.[6]

To boil down this quote to its essence, it tells us that scientists do not really know how abiogenesis happened, yet they are convinced it happened. Life arose from nonliving matter, though the forces and processes that created the cell and gave it the ability to replicate are "still a mystery."

In a blog article on the *Scientific American* website titled "Pssst! Don't Tell the Creationists, but Scientists Don't Have a Clue How Life Began," science writer John Horgan addresses some of the extreme difficulties involved even in theorizing how abiogenesis occurred. He notes that after a conference of geologists, chemists, astronomers, and biologists at Arizona State University, the participants emerged "as stumped as ever by the riddle of life."[7] The problems involved are so enormous that Chris McKay of NASA's Ames Research Center says that "there is not even a consensus on how to approach the problem."[8]

Harvard chemist George M. Whitesides, recipient of the Priestley Medal, the highest honor given by the American Chemical Society, says this about the origin of life: "This problem is one of the big ones in science. . . . Most chemists believe, as do I, that life emerged spontaneously from mixtures of molecules in the prebiotic Earth. How? I have no idea."[9]

We can see that the claim that life on earth emerged from nonliving matter is merely a belief. Scientific support for the theory is utterly absent. The phenomenon of life emerging from nonliving matter has never in history been witnessed, nor has the theory been confirmed by scientific experiment, though such confirmation has often been attempted. Biologists such as Stanley Miller, Harold Urey, and Sydney W.

Fox have tried to replicate the conditions and the sequence of events that might have caused organic cells to be randomly assembled and then spontaneously shocked to life. Yet no one has ever been able to create a single organic cell or bring a dead cell to life even under the most carefully controlled laboratory conditions.

The famous Miller-Urey experiment followed the long-held belief that life began in a "primordial soup" containing just the right chemicals to produce preliving cells. The experiment did produce amino acids (which is now deemed so simple that it's done even in high school biology classes), but it failed to achieve its goal.[10] The fact remains that no viable mechanism has been discovered that could have produced the hypothesized primordial life-fostering soup or assembled life-supporting cells.

If you have ever had to draw or label an organic cell diagram in science class, you know that there is nothing simple about simple cells. The fact is, these student drawings do not even scratch the surface of the actual mind-boggling complexity of a living cell. Cells are structured to support life. They contain specialized parts called organelles that function to keep the cells alive. Organelles perform much like human organs. They govern ingestion and elimination and power the cell with energy. Each organelle performs its own special, coordinated function that is vital to maintaining the cell's life. These organelles would be meaningless unless cells were meant to bear life. For the preliving cell to possess parts specifically structured to support life before life existed would require evolution to anticipate life during the formation of cellular structures. This would force naturalists to attribute something like mind and purpose to evolution, attributes that they necessarily deny. We will take a closer look at this in the next chapter, but to think that random nature would blindly assemble a cell specifically structured with all the complex paraphernalia to support life when no such thing as life previously existed defies logic.

An alternate theory for abiogenesis suggests that life began in the sea near a hypothermal vent. But the National Academy of Sciences refutes both this theory and the "primordial soup" theory that undergirds the Miller-Urey experiment, saying, "Two amino acids do not spontaneously join in water. Rather, the opposite reaction is thermodynamically favored."[11] Water breaks down protein chains, making it virtually impossible for life to begin in a water-based environment—which invalidates both the primordial soup and the hypothermic vent theories.

The Chicken-Egg Conundrum of the Genetic Code

Another insurmountable problem for abiogenesis is that unguided natural processes cannot explain the origin of the genetic code. Science writer Casey Luskin of *Evolution News* explains the problem by comparing the genetic code to a DVD:

> DVDs are rich in information, but without the machinery of a DVD player to read the disk, process

its information, and convert it into a picture and sound, the disk would be useless. But what if the instructions for building the first DVD player were only found encoded on a DVD? You could never play the DVD to learn how to build a DVD player.[12]

This analogy describes the information contained in the genetic code. Like a DVD, the genetic code is useless without a reader mechanism. But the formation of the reader mechanism is guided by instructions embedded in the code itself. As Luskin goes on to say:

In living cells, information-carrying molecules (such as DNA or RNA) are like the DVD, and the cellular machinery that reads that information and converts it into proteins is like the DVD player. . . . Yet in cells, the machines required for processing the genetic information in RNA or DNA are encoded by those same genetic molecules—they perform and direct the very task that builds them.[13]

It's the chicken-egg conundrum. The DNA molecule carries the instructions for building the cellular structures to read and activate all DNA information. Both the information and the reader are required to exist simultaneously. Since DNA needs proteins and proteins need DNA, which came first? How could either exist without the other?

Physical chemist and Nobel Prize winner Dr. Harold

Urey, who participated in the Miller-Urey attempt to generate life in the laboratory, says this: "All of us who study the origin of life find that the more we look into it, the more we feel it is too complex to have evolved anywhere. We all believe as an article of faith that life evolved from dead matter on this planet. It is just that its complexity is so great, it is hard for us to imagine that it did."[14]

We find Dr. Urey's statement to be fairly astounding. He admits that he has come to realize life is too complex to have evolved from dead matter, yet he continues to believe it did. Furthermore, he admits that he believes it solely "as an article of faith." He has neither proof nor a viable theory. Theists find it incredible that naturalistic scientists who are so baffled by the enigma of life's origins refuse even to consider the possibility of an intelligent creator. It seems clear that all the evidence presented by science, experience, and common sense shows us plainly and without exception that life comes only from preexisting life. This inevitably means a totally naturalistic universe that begins with nothing but nonliving, inorganic elements will remain forever nonliving and inorganic. How can one believe otherwise without turning a rational, foundational principle of science on its head?

If we reject the theory that life arose from nonliving matter, it means that since life exists, some self-existent life must necessarily have been present from infinity. Theists can no more explain how this is possible than naturalists can explain how life arose via abiogenesis. According to the logic and data available to the human mind, life could neither have begun on its own *nor* existed forever. For life to exist at all seems impossible. Yet life exists. We contend that attributing its existence to an eternally living, ultra-intelligent being is at least as reasonable as thinking it arose spontaneously from dead matter. As British writer G. K. Chesterton says, "It is absurd for the Evolutionist to complain that it is unthinkable for an admittedly unthinkable God to make everything out of nothing and then pretend that it is more thinkable that nothing should turn itself into everything."[15]

The Fatal Problems with Naturalistic Origin Theories

Neither of the naturalistic theories of origins—the big bang or abiogenesis—could have occurred unless the natural laws governing the universe were suspended. Both the big bang and abiogenesis require the occurrence of the following four events, each of which violates verified scientific laws. The big bang and abiogenesis could be true explanations for the origin of the universe and for life only under the following conditions:

- Nothing produced something.
- Chaos produced order.
- Death produced life.
- Simplicity produced complexity.

No one has ever observed any of these four processes happening; science cannot induce them to happen; and reason says they cannot happen. Yet the naturalistic theories of origins can be true only if they did happen.

The underlying philosophy driving naturalism is that nature is all there is. There is no god. The universe is a self-existent, self-created machine. Life emerged from dead matter on its own, and as we will discuss in the next chapter, all living species developed by evolving from simple organisms into creatures of greater complexity and acquired the ability to reason through mindless processes that defy known scientific laws.

These foundation blocks of naturalistic origins have no credible scientific bedrock. They are fatally flawed philosophies because they are not based on sound reasoning or verified science. Naturalists ask us to believe that something can be generated from nothing, existence can arise naturally from nonexistence, order can emerge from chaos, life from nonlife, diversity from singularity, and mind from mindlessness. They see the universe as an engine that assembled itself and started up on an empty tank with no hand to turn the key. You may recall from your high school science classes that such things cannot happen. Both science and reason agree (as true science and true reason always do) that no effect can be greater than its cause. A baseball hurled from the pitcher's hand at eighty miles per hour will not pick up speed and cross the plate at ninety miles per hour. A rubber ball will not bounce higher than the point from which you drop it. You can't feed a hen one pound of grain and expect her to lay two pounds of eggs. The output cannot be greater than the input. The rigid laws of cause and effect govern all the natural activity in the universe. Yet naturalism asks us to suspend reason and even science to assume that exceptions have occurred despite the fact that no exception has ever been observed or demonstrated.

Science is incapable of discovering the source of origins because science is by definition limited to the study of nature, and the source of nature must necessarily precede the existence of nature. This means the forces and events that generated matter and life are outside nature and therefore beyond the reach of scientific inquiry. We have no way to get testable data on these first causes because they occurred prior to the possibility of observation.

Even Stephen Hawking, in explaining his theory that the universe came into existence from nothing, expressed the futility of science trying to probe the nothingness that existed prior to the moment the universe created itself. He compared its beginnings to the south pole, picturing longitude lines radiating out from the pole as the universe's expansion. Then he added, "To ask what happened before the beginning of the universe would become a meaningless question, because there is nothing south of the South Pole."[16]

Using Hawking's own logic, we can say that for scientists to declare that God did not create the universe is an indefensible claim because science itself—which is the study of nature—did not exist until nature began. This means— as Hawking points out—that there was no mechanism for observing what existed prior to the universe and therefore no justification for asserting that there was "nothing south of the South Pole."

We can see that the question of origins is not scientific at all; it is *metaphysical*. The only avenues for approaching the subject are either religion or philosophy simply because the question of origins takes us inevitably outside the realm of nature and thus outside the realm of science.

We must appreciate open and honest scientists who are willing to admit that many of their assumptions are philosophical and not scientific. One example is the internationally renowned astrophysicist George F. R. Ellis, who said this:

> People need to be aware that there is a range of models that could explain the observations [of scientists]. . . . For instance, I can construct you a spherically symmetrical universe with Earth at its center, and you cannot disprove it based on observations. . . . You can only exclude it on philosophical grounds. In my view there is absolutely nothing wrong in that. What I want to bring into the open is the fact that we are using philosophical criteria in choosing our models. A lot of cosmology tries to hide that.[17]

Why Nature Cannot Originate Anything

The cold, hard fact that undermines naturalism is that the laws of nature cannot account for origins. This we know to be true because the laws of nature never cause anything to happen. They merely describe what happens after an event is caused or set in motion.

To explain this fact, C. S. Lewis supposes a set of billiard balls resting on a table in a seagoing ship. A lurch in the ship sets a ball in motion, causing it to strike a second ball. He explains that the lurch in the ship that set the original ball in motion was caused by a wave, which was set in motion by other waves, which were set in motion by natural phenomena such as winds and tides.

Then Lewis points out that all these movements, once set in motion, could be described by the rigid laws of nature—their direction, their speed, their momentum, and the momentum lost and gained by the collision of the balls. None of these measurable facts, however, were *caused* by the laws of nature. Then he gives us this startling but inevitable conclusion: "*In the whole history of the universe, the laws of Nature have never produced a single event.* They are the pattern to which every event must conform, provided only that it can be induced to happen. But how do you get it to do that? . . . The laws of Nature can give you no help there" (italics in the original).[18]

The point: looking to the laws of nature as the cause of anything is futile. The laws of nature never cause anything. All causes must be fed into the system of nature. Trace the causes that moved the billiard ball back through all the stages—the lurch of the ship, the wave, the wind, the motion of the earth, the gravity of the moon, the energy from the sun, the forces that formed the sun—and eventually you get to the beginning of the universe where all causes had to originate. Could the laws of nature have originated the universe? No, nature itself was originated at the beginning of the universe. Nature and its laws were the *result* of origination, not its cause. Whatever existed prior to nature originated the matter and energy that became nature, but that prenatural cause had to be outside nature, and thus it is what we call *supernatural.* Once nature was created and energy was fed into it, the laws of nature could be used to describe the resulting movements but not their origins.

The Emperor's New Clothes

You may remember Hans Christian Andersen's famous story "The Emperor's New Clothes." In this pointed tale, two tailors make a magical new suit for an emperor. They claim the suit will be invisible to anyone who is incompetent, stupid, or disloyal to the king. In reality, however, the tailors make no clothes at all. Instead, they pretend to dress the king with an elaborate new suit and make the people believe the suit is invisible to them. So when the emperor wears his new suit in public, all the people are afraid to admit that they do not see the suit on him. They are intimidated, afraid to be thought stupid or incompetent. Then an innocent but shocked little boy points to the emperor and says, "He doesn't have any clothes on at all!" Immediately the people know they have been duped by intimidation and peer pressure into believing something untrue.

The naturalistic explanations of origins are the emperor's new clothes. Many people believe these theories because they are proclaimed to be the underlying truths and supporting pillars for our secular age. It is easy for those of us who are not scientists to feel intimidated by naturalism's claims, especially since they dominate the major institutions of our present culture. The books, articles, and blogs explaining naturalistic theories are usually well-crafted, and on the surface they seem plausible to readers who do not dig too deeply. When we read detailed accounts of the expansion and organization of the primeval singularity into specific forms, the conditions and processes by which cells formed and came alive, and the evolutionary fundamentals of natural selection, mutations, and the dating and interpretation of fossils, it's easy to be impressed. It's easy to say, "These folks are highly educated, and they all seem to agree, so they must be right."

We must be vigilant to note that beneath the technical verbiage within these stories, there are no objective, verified evidences supporting their major claims. We realize that is a bold statement, but we urge you to test it for yourself. The explanations offered by scientists are merely the foliage of theories that are fatally diseased at the root. They do not address the central reasoning flaws that undermine naturalistic explanations. They are contrary to what true science demonstrates to be inviolable truths. These truths are as follows:

- Nothing can never produce anything.
- Chaos can never produce order.
- Death can never produce life.
- Simplicity can never produce complexity.

We theists believe in all four of these scientific principles, which were taught to us in our school science classes. Naturalists say that we are flouting science when we will not concede to theoretical exceptions to immutable scientific laws. We are depicted as being antiscience when, in fact, we often find it to be the other way around. It is because of our deep respect for science that we question naturalism which, as we have demonstrated, relies on unobserved and unproven exceptions to established science to validate its theories of origins. As we continue exploring these theories with a look at the origin of the species, we trust that you will judge for yourself who is departing from true science.

QUESTIONS FOR THOUGHT AND DISCUSSION

1. Why doesn't the big bang theory explain the origin of matter?

2. What is the primary flaw in the abiogenesis claim that life arose from nonliving material?

3. Why is it illogical to think evolution could produce a nonliving cell that could bear life?

4. Why can't the laws of nature explain origins?

5. What is meant by the assertion that naturalism is a philosophy and not a science?

6. What are the four central flaws of naturalistic theories of origins? Why do you think people are more willing to overlook these flaws than to consider the possibility that God exists?

7. How can believers in creation claim to support science while claiming naturalists do not?

THE HOTEL THAT CHARLIE BUILT

*Is one of secularism's foundational structures
beginning to crumble?*

For many years, Charlie lived in a hotel. It was the only one in town, and it was owned by a non-resident landlord who hired local managers to run it. The hotel was clean, well-respected, well-kept, and rock-solid. Yet despite these assets, Charlie thought it was regrettably old-fashioned and needed serious updating. The landlord, however, had no intention of making changes.

So Charlie decided to build his own hotel. He bought a parcel of land near the river. It was easily accessible to the town and filled with trees, birds, flowers, and lush grass. He drew up an elaborate, innovative design and built his hotel. It was an immediate hit. Many guests left the old hotel and flocked to Charlie's. Many townspeople even sold their houses and moved into Charlie's hotel.

The hotel became a showplace and source of pride for the town. Newspapers and magazines praised it. Books were written about it. It soon became the new standard for what hotels ought to be. Charlie became famous.

Unfortunately, Charlie didn't realize that the land he had built on was unstable. It had once been a swampland, and there was no bedrock beneath it. Cracks began to appear in the hotel's floors and walls. The roof began to leak. Charlie hired workers to paper over cracks and reinforce the tilting walls and sagging ceilings. But the more they patched, the more breaches appeared, and the building began to creak and tremble.

Few guests moved out, however. They were so enamored of the hotel's innovative design that they chose to stay and help Charlie with the patching and buttressing. Many even donated new materials to support the sagging beams and plaster over the expanding cracks. Journalists and authors who had staked their professional reputations on the hotel refused to report its flaws. When questions arose, they insisted the hotel was in perfect shape.

Charlie's hotel is still standing, though its precarious condition is now clearly visible to many.

Some say it could collapse at any moment.

No doubt you quickly recognized that this little parable is about Charles Darwin (Charlie) and his theory of evolution (the hotel). Of course, we have carefully constructed it to portray our own perspective on that theory. We fully understand that you may disagree with our characterization, thinking as so many do that evolution is settled science and any challenge to it displays sheer ignorance or quackery. In fact, you might counter our view with your own challenge, asking this perfectly reasonable question: If the theory of evolution is indeed as weak and riddled with fatal flaws as we claim, how did it become so dominant, and why does it continue to stand?

It's true that evolution has become dominant. In most official institutions, evolution has replaced creation as the preferred explanation for the origin of species and has become the home of many looking for an alternative to theism. But unless you closely follow the controversies debated within the scientific community, you may not be aware that advances in scientific knowledge have shown evolution to be so riddled with inconsistencies that many of its weaknesses have become glaringly apparent, even to staunch evolutionists. Yet the theory is still doggedly propped up and vehemently defended.

Why?

In this chapter we will address this question and others that keep arising about the viability of the theory of evolution. It is not within the scope of this book to present a thorough refutation of this theory, but it is so pervasive and so often used to discredit belief in God that we feel a need to explore at least a few of the major logical and scientific problems that undermine its claims.

How Did Evolution Get Its Foothold?

Charles Darwin first proposed the theory of evolution in his book *On the Origin of Species*, published in 1859. It caught the imagination of influential, nineteenth-century thinkers such as Thomas Huxley, George Bernard Shaw, and others who found in it a respectable intellectual prop for atheism. God was no longer needed to explain the variety of life on the planet. Scientists in many fields quickly adopted the theory and drew it under the umbrella of science despite its lack of empirical evidence and normal scientific testing.

Evolution did not penetrate the wall of religion, however, until after the widely publicized 1925 Scopes "Monkey Trial" in Dayton, Tennessee. That trial came about when the ACLU, looking for a way to challenge a Tennessee law against teaching evolution in public schools, convinced high school teacher John Scopes to introduce evolution in a science classroom. Though the ACLU lost the trial, heavily biased reporting by agnostic journalist H. L. Mencken did much to give evolution positive exposure.

Soon the theory rolled into the mainstream of popular thought on wheels oiled by the growing prestige of science. Science had gained almost godlike status with its twentieth-century cornucopia of medicines and conveniences and with the spectacular success of space exploration. With major disciplines of science incorporating the theory, much of the general public blindly fell in step.

This sea change of public opinion gave secularists the

opportunity to maneuver the religious explanation of origins—and religion in general, particularly Christianity—out of public schools. As a result, evolution is now firmly embedded in public education, most universities, the media, government, law courts, and entertainment.

Evolution's domination of the West's most influential institutions has emboldened naturalists to make unsubstantiated claims with impunity. Despite the lack of confirming evidence and scientific testing, they now assert that evolution is a certified, scientific truth. Even back in 2002 a cover story of *U.S. News and World Report* stated: "By now, scientists say, evolution is no longer 'just a theory.' It's an everyday phenomenon, a fundamental fact of biology as real as hunger and as unavoidable as death."[1]

A Macro Conclusion from a Micro Premise

As a proof that evolution is a fact, naturalists point to how selective breeding produces varied strains of animals and how colors and appendages of animals in the wild adapt to their environments. You may recall Darwin's study of finches in the Galápagos Islands. He observed how finch beaks adapted to changing environmental conditions. In periods of drought, when finches were forced to dig deeper for food, their beaks grew longer. Darwin theorized that natural selection produced this change. When a finch pair with longer beaks mated, they passed that characteristic to their offspring, which survived better than the offspring of birds with shorter beaks. Thus, in time, the longer-beaked birds dominated the finch population in a given locality.

Theists do not deny the obvious process of adaptation within species, or *microevolution*. Our objection arises when evolutionists make the broad, unwarranted jump to claiming adaptive changes within species as evidence for changes from one species to another, or *macroevolution*.

University of California law professor Dr. Phillip E. Johnson has shown that this conclusion is too broad to be justified by its limited premise. "Evolutionary biologists are not content merely to explain how variation occurs within limits," Johnson says. "They aspire to answer a much broader question: how complex organisms like birds and flowers and human beings came into existence in the first place." Johnson goes on to say, "Neo-Darwinian evolution in this broad sense is a philosophical doctrine so lacking in empirical support that [Harvard professor] Stephen Jay Gould once pronounced it in a reckless moment to be 'effectively dead.'"[2]

The claim that evolution is no longer a mere theory but a fact is another illegitimate jump. True science does not elevate a theory to the level of fact without empirical evidence or replicable experiment. The authentic scientific process starts with a hypothesis, tests it by experimentation and observation, and then either abandons it for lack of evidence or reports the evidences that certify it as demonstrable science. This process has never occurred with evolution. In fact, it cannot occur. There is no time machine that can take scientists back to witness the change from one species to another, no experiment that has replicated species evolution, and no fossil evidence that validates it.

Dr. George G. Simpson, called the most influential paleontologist of the twentieth century, said, "It is inherent in any definition of science that statements that cannot be checked by observation are not really about anything . . . or at the very least, they are not science."[3] This means evolution is not authentic science. It remains a mere theory.

To create a rationale for these and other unproven evolutionary jumps, naturalists devise what some call "just-so" stories. For example, a University of California, Berkeley, website explains how birds evolved after small dinosaurs developed feathers for insulating their bodies and warming their eggs:

> Many of their bones were reduced and fused, which
> may have helped increase the efficiency of flight.
> Similarly, the bone walls became even thinner,
> and the feathers became longer and their vanes
> asymmetrical, probably also improving flight. The
> bony tail was reduced to a stump, and a spray of
> feathers at the tail eventually took on the function
> of improving stability and maneuverability. The
> wishbone, which was present in non-bird dinosaurs,
> became stronger and more elaborate, and the bones
> of the shoulder girdle evolved to connect to the
> breastbone, anchoring the flight apparatus of the
> forelimb. The breastbone itself became larger, and

evolved a central keel along the midline of the breast which served to anchor the flight muscles. The arms evolved to be longer than the legs, as the main form of locomotion switched from running to flight.[4]

This story exudes the aura of science and credibility. Notice, however, that it cites no scientific evidence whatsoever as to how any of the steps from dinosaur to bird occurred. Nor is evidence available elsewhere. This is pure speculation—merely a just-so story and nothing more.

Before his death, evolutionist Dr. Colin Patterson, senior paleontologist at the British Museum of Natural History, seemed to be waking up to the weaknesses that abound in the theory of evolution. He wrote, "The secular myths of evolution have had a damaging effect on scientific research, leading to distortion, to needless controversy, and to gross misuse of science. . . . I mean the stories, the narratives about change over time; how the dinosaurs became extinct; how the mammals evolved; where man came from. These seem to me to be little more than story-telling."[5]

Check for yourself, and you will see that certified evidence is the one thing you will never find in scientists' accounts of how evolution works.

The Fallacy of the Fossils

For their primary support of evolution, paleontologists have long relied on the fossil record—but fossil evidence is also based on unsupported stories formulated to support their theories. The fossils themselves display no inherent characteristics to suggest that they are links in evolutionary ancestral lines. One must first believe that evolution is a fact to have any reason to interpret a particular fossil as a stage in the process.

Many evolutionary scientists have come to realize that contrivances abound in fossil stories and have begun to dismiss fossils as valid evidence for evolution. The questionable nature of fossil evidence has been apparent for many decades. In fact, troubling questions began with Charles Darwin himself. He was baffled by the utter absence of fossil evidence for transitions between species. He said, "As by this theory, innumerable transitional forms must have existed, why do we not find them embedded in countless numbers in the crust of the earth?"[6]

Ninety years after Darwin wrote his book, problems still persisted in fossil evidence. In 1949 Cambridge geologist Dr. Robert H. Rastall wrote this about the questionable methods of identification and dating of fossils:

It cannot be denied that from a strictly philosophical standpoint geologists are here arguing in a circle. The succession of organisms has been determined by a study of their remains embedded in the rocks, and the relative ages of the rocks are determined by the remains of organisms that they contain.[7]

As Dr. Rastall tells us, fossils are interpreted as evidence of the theory by using the assumptions of the theory as the starting point. The result is a *tautology*—a closed circle of logic with no foundational premise. It works like this: "We know evolution occurs because we have found the fossils of evolving species. We know these are fossils of evolving species because we know evolution occurs." The fact that fossils of some extinct species bear similarities to present-day creatures does not prove or even suggest ancestry. To claim otherwise is to make an unwarranted leap to a predetermined conclusion.

Evolutionists have long been baffled by the layer of the earth's crust laid down in the Cambrian era, which is filled with fossils of creatures that suddenly appeared on the scene fully developed and with no evidence of ancestors in the strata beneath. Richard Dawkins wrote, "It is as though they were just planted there, without any evolutionary history."[8]

Fossil evidence is as absent today as it was in both Darwin's and Rastall's time, which is causing many scientists to have second thoughts. Oxford zoologist Mark Ridley concluded that "no real evolutionist . . . uses the fossil record as evidence in favour of the theory of evolution as opposed to special creation."[9]

In his book *Evolution of Living Organisms*, French paleontologist Pierre-Paul Grassé states:

From the almost total absence of fossil evidence . . .
it follows that any explanation of the mechanism in
the creative evolution of the fundamental structural

JOSH McDOWELL AND THOMAS WILLIAMS

plans is heavily burdened with hypothesis. . . . The
lack of direct evidence leads to the formulation of
pure conjecture as to the genesis of the phyla; we
do not even have a basis to determine the extent to
which these opinions are correct.[10]

Dr. Colin Patterson was asked by a fellow scientist to
defend his lack of illustrations for transitional fossils in his
book *Evolution*. In a letter he replied, "If I knew of any, fossil
or living, I would certainly have included them. You suggest
that an artist should be used to visualize such transforma-
tions, but where would he get the information from? I could
not, honestly, provide it, and if I were to leave it to artistic
license, would that not mislead the reader?"[11]

Yet despite the diminishing credibility of the fossil record,
many evolutionary scientists cling doggedly to fossils as support for the theory, using creative stories to justify their continued use as evidence. When accumulating facts discredit
one story, another can be devised to replace it. For example,
when Harvard paleontologist Stephen Jay Gould grew frus-
trated with the lack of fossil evidence for evolution, he and
fellow scientist Niles Eldredge created a new story which they
called *punctuated equilibrium*. They proposed that evolutionary changes did not happen gradually over long periods of
time, as Darwinians thought. Instead, species populations
remained stable for millions of years, and then a small, isolated segment of the species mutated suddenly. The segment's smallness and isolation combined with the quickness

of the process rendered fossilization unlikely. What evidence did Gould offer to verify his new theory? None. It was just another story contrived to prop up Charlie's hotel as the pillar of fossil evidence collapsed.

Evolution's Headache: The Origin of Sex

What is the evolutionary explanation of sex? Naturalists tell us that the first living cells arose via abiogenesis and began to reproduce by mitosis, or cell division. In time, some cells began to replicate themselves by sexual pairing. How did this radical change come about? Here is one naturalist's explanation:

> Sexual reproduction began without sexually distinct
> organs, and then such organs evolved in tandem over
> time. Many plants, for example, are hermaphroditic:
> each plant has both male and female sexual organs.
> But the first sexually reproducing organisms were
> a form of single-celled bacterium which thus had
> no organs at all. As sexually reproducing organisms
> evolved into multicellular forms and their cells began
> to specialize, some cells began specializing for male
> and female reproductive function, both evolving at
> the same time, by small gradual steps.[12]

Vague, general explanations such as this seem plausible until you start thinking about the details. The writer of this just-so story does not begin to address the extreme complexity

involved in making the transition from asexual to sexual reproduction even in its simplest, most rudimentary form. Though
he claims his two theoretical bacteria had no complementary
sexual organs, they must necessarily have developed *separately
yet simultaneously* the capacity to produce complementary
gametes—forerunners of male sperm and female ova—the
sexually differentiated cells required to create a separate new
organism. Though he says the first sexual bacterium had no
organs at all, it must have had some sort of mechanism for
delivering the sexually differentiated seminal substance to
achieve the merging that results in reproduction—some system capable of transferring the male gamete to the female.
Before the first incidence of sexual reproduction could occur,
all these factors had to be in place with the gametes of both
sexes pre-equipped with the separate but complementary
components required to create a third organism. To produce
such a highly complex system requiring so many match-
ing chemicals and parts, evolution would have had to "look
ahead" and prepare apparatus in advance to accommodate
that first, rudimentary event of sexual reproduction. As we
said in the last chapter, this would suggest a mind and purpose
behind random nature, which evolutionists would deny.

That's only the beginning of the difficulty. As these rudimentary organisms evolved into more complex creatures,
both the male and female systems had to evolve simultaneously at each stage of advancement and yet remain consistently complementary. This difficulty looms even larger
when you realize that evolutionary theory relies heavily on

mutation as the process that produces the most dramatic changes in a species. Mutations possess two characteristics that work against their ability to evolve separate but complementary sexual systems. First, mutations always occur as the result of damage to DNA and thus are inadequate to explain advancement in body parts or functions. Second, with the possible exception in certain protected regions of the DNA chain (as tentatively suggested by recent plant research[13]), mutations are always random. That means these separate sexual systems—male and female—must have evolved in all species through consistent random mutations that occurred simultaneously and somehow managed to match each other by recreating complementarity at every stage of development. (Apparently, we must ignore the fact that it's impossible for an event to be both random and consistently simultaneous.)

These monumental—we will go so far as to say insurmountable—difficulties explain why Graham Bell, in his book *The Masterpiece of Nature: The Evolution of Genetics and Sexuality*, says that "sex is the queen of problems in evolutionary biology. . . . The insights of Darwin and Mendel, which have illuminated so many mysteries, have so far failed to shed more than a dim and wavering light on the central mystery of sexuality."[14]

As another science writer puts it: "The origin and subsequent maintenance of sex and recombination is a phenomenon not easily explained by Darwinian evolution. . . . To believe that purely materialistic processes, governed by the laws of chance, could have produced such a mechanism stretches credulity beyond reasonable limits."[15]

The Marvel of Making Babies

If sex is a mystery inexplicable by evolutionary processes, what happens as a result of sex is even more mind-boggling. We're referring to the unparalleled marvel of a new human created within the womb of a female. Consider the extreme complexity involved in the process. An ovum is impregnated by a sperm and divides into two cells, then four, then eight, and so on until the cells begin to differentiate and form limbs, fingers, toes, bones, muscles, skin, teeth, hair, vertebrae, fingernails, eyes, sixty thousand miles of veins and capillaries, DNA chains, a beating heart, a brain, and many more organs and glands of extreme complexity.

No matter how contrived a story naturalists develop to explain how mindless evolution could instigate and perpetuate this immensely involved and intricate process, is there any reasonable alternative to the necessity that purpose and intelligence had to be involved?

Irreducible Complexity: Can Evolution Plan Ahead?

Biochemist Dr. Michael Behe caused a stir among evolutionists with his book *Darwin's Black Box* when he pointed out that most of the organs in animal bodies are what he calls "irreducibly complex." Evolutionary mechanisms are inadequate to explain complex bodily structures because all parts of each structure must be complete and functioning before they have meaning. They would be unable to function and thus useless while their component parts were evolving. How would evolution "know" to keep these structures evolving toward a specific function throughout millions of years of uselessness?

Dr. Behe illustrates the principle with a common mousetrap. None of its five parts—base, swatter, bait holder, trigger, and spring—is functional without the other parts. They must all be intact, fully formed, operative, and in place for the mousetrap to work. He then applies this principle to the human eye. The necessary parts of the eye—lens, cornea, iris, retina, fluids, and optic nerve—would be of no use without the other parts. While evolving, these separate components would be useless. To maintain the development of these parts through their nonfunctional stages would require evolution to anticipate their eventual use. This, again, would have the effect of attributing mind and purpose to the process of evolution—attributes which naturalists necessarily deny.

For the past decade and a half, irreducible complexity has put the evolutionary community in a dither. It has yet to be successfully refuted.[16]

Evolution: The Naturalist's God

The challenge of irreducible complexity highlights a characteristic of evolution that its proponents seem unable to acknowledge. They insist that evolution is mindless and has no purpose, but this is clearly not the case. Evolution as conceived reveals a definite purpose and thus possesses attributes that can be ascribed only to a mind. Evolution clearly favors life over nonlife, and everything attributed to it reveals the advancement and enhancement of life to be its underlying purpose. Life in its early stages was much too fragile to survive without evolution's nudge. If evolution is truly mindless, how could it have stepped in and provided these nudges that consistently favor survival over nonsurvival? The law of probability would dictate that at some of these stages, evolution mindlessly would have allowed death to obliterate life. But when it comes to evolution, the law of probability is placed off limits.

To demonstrate that naturalists do believe evolution favors survival, look at some of their just-so stories:

- They tell us that evolution formed an extremely complex cell that would support all the coordinated functions of life *even before life existed.*
- Next, evolution created a mechanism for the reproduction of life, though there was no need or reason for life to continue.
- Then evolution employed mechanisms such as natural selection, adaptation, and mutation to improve life, and added complexity to enhance the survival of life, at each stage of development.

We are told, of course, that each of these advancements was truly random and could as easily have gone the other way—but the principle of random chance confutes this. It says that at each of the millions of stages of its advancement, life should at times have been overtaken by the mindless failure of evolution to provide the next needed nudge. It's as if at each of these developmental stages, a coin was flipped and each time it landed on "heads." We've all tossed coins enough to know that random chance would never allow such a thing to happen.

A central but seemingly hushed-up principle of evolution is that it consistently favors life and acts to move it forward. The theory may have been conceived as a mindless mechanism devised merely to explain the random development of life, but its proponents soon had to slip into its attributes the element of purpose. For example, an article describing a recent discovery in the genetics of the weed known as thale cress said that "the plant has evolved to protect its genes from mutation to ensure survival."[17] Here, as in so many similar statements in scientific writing, the purpose of evolution is plainly revealed—to protect life and ensure its survival. Evolution has become the secularist's overarching explanation not only for the origin of the species, but also for the deliberate advancement and preservation of life.

It seems that naturalists manage to hide from themselves the fact that for evolution to work, it must necessarily take on the creative aspects of a god. Indeed, we would suggest that the concept of evolution exists only because naturalists need an alternative to God that displays all of his creative attributes. It could not do the things attributed to it without supernatural powers that nature itself does not possess.

Perhaps you wonder if we are overstating the way naturalists inadvertently think of evolution. We don't think so. Naturalists attribute to evolution creative powers and acts that nature has never been known to perform and cannot perform. As demonstrated by C. S. Lewis's explanation of the limits of cause and effect quoted in the previous chapter, nature never originates anything.

DNA and the Impossibility of Information Evolution

In 1953 James Watson and Francis Crick discovered within the nucleus of living cells the genetic structure deoxyribonucleic acid, commonly known as DNA. After more than a half century, the code embedded within DNA has been deciphered. It was found that the infinitesimal double-helix molecule—less than two-millionths of a millimeter thick—contains information recorded in a "language" consisting of *three billion genetic letters*. According to Dr. Stephen Meyer, director of the Center for Science and Culture at the Discovery Institute, "One of the most extraordinary discoveries of the twentieth century was that DNA actually stores information—the detailed instructions for assembling proteins—in the form of a four-character digital code."[18] DNA contains detailed instructions for assembling every living creature on earth. It would require more than 380 books, each the size of an *Encyclopedia Britannica* volume, to contain the amount of information stored in a single DNA molecule.

It is impossible to overstate the order and complexity of this information. According to Dr. Meyer, "The coding regions of DNA have *exactly* the same relevant properties as a computer code or language."[19] This means DNA possesses the equivalent to grammar, punctuation, correct spelling, syntax, and an objective to be communicated.

To realize the impact of DNA on evolution, it is important to recognize that information and matter are two altogether separate categories. Information is communicated through matter, but it is not matter. A book composed of paper, binding, and ink conveys information, but the book itself is not information. The information is independent of the book and could also be conveyed orally or through handwriting, an audio recording, a digital reader, or a video. Information is something altogether separate from the physical medium that contains it. Similarly, the information stored within the DNA molecule is independent of the matter that makes up the molecule itself.

Darwin's theory does not account for the presence of coded information embedded in the body's cells. In his day it was thought that a cell was little more than a simple blob of dough-like protoplasm. Now we know that it contains all the complexity of a metropolitan city or even a universe. Darwinism bases evolution on life arising from organic matter and makes no accommodation for precisely coded information embedded within matter.

At the base of this naturalistic dilemma is the fact that—as virtually everyone recognizes—precise, organized information must always be the product of intelligence. This throws a monkey wrench into evolution's gears. As Lee Strobel writes, "No hypothesis has come close to explaining how information got into biological matter by naturalistic means."[20] No one can explain how megacomplex, organized, precise, and meaningful information could have been created by random chance.

A species' characteristics are dictated by the information stored in the DNA molecule. For Darwinian evolution to create a new species with added characteristics means a mutation must add new information to the DNA chain. The problem is that there is no known mechanism to provide that increase. Biophysicist Dr. Lee Spetner explains the problem as it relates to the neo-Darwinian claim that birds evolved from reptiles: "Reptiles have no genetic information for wings or feathers." He goes on to say that changing a reptile into a bird would require the addition of new and complex information to the DNA, which the Darwinian model cannot account for: "And not only is it improbable on the mathematical level, that is theoretically, but experimentally one has not found a single mutation that one can point at that actually adds information. In fact, every beneficial mutation that I have seen reduces the information, it loses information."[21] Here Spetner's statement squares with the known scientific principle that mutations only occur when DNA is damaged and left unrepaired, which means the general effect of mutation tends to be destructive rather than creative. This principle underscores the premise of Dr. Michael Behe's book *Darwin Devolves*. He demonstrates that evolutionary changes do not occur by adding information to organisms, but solely by subtracting it. This suggests that a more accurate name for evolution might be devolution.[22]

According to Dr. Meyer, "Evolutionists are still trying to apply Darwin's nineteenth-century thinking to a twenty-first-century reality, and it's not working. . . . I think the information revolution taking place in biology is sounding the death knell for Darwinism and chemical evolutionary theories."[23]

Growing Doubts and Defections

Considering the accumulating weaknesses of evolution, several scientists in various fields have begun to express doubts about the authenticity of the theory. Prominent physicist and mathematician Dr. Wolfgang Smith said, "A growing number of respectable scientists are defecting from the evolutionist camp. . . . For the most part these 'experts' have abandoned Darwinism, not on the basis of religious faith or biblical persuasions, but on strictly scientific grounds, and in some instances, regretfully."[24]

Wolfgang Smith's claim that a "growing number" of scientists are now defecting from Darwinism is no mere hyperbole.

In 2001, the Discovery Institute launched a website that they named "A Scientific Dissent from Darwinism." The website posted the following statement, which was initially signed by several prominent scientists: "We are skeptical of claims for the ability of random mutation and natural selection to account for the complexity of life. Careful examination of the evidence for Darwinian theory should be encouraged."[25] As of May 2021, the statement had been signed by 1,187 leaders in scientific fields, including many prominent and well-known names. According to the website, "The list is growing and includes scientists from the US National Academy of Sciences, Russian, Hungarian and Czech National Academies, as well as from universities such as Yale, Princeton, Stanford, MIT, UC Berkeley, UCLA, and others."[26]

Yet despite the growing number of scientists awakening to evolution's deficiencies, the theory remains by far the dominant view of most naturalists today. If the theory is as weak and lacking in evidence as we and the scientists we've quoted claim, the natural question is, why does the vast majority of the scientific community cling to it so tenaciously?

Why Do Naturalists Cling to a Failing Theory?

One reason may be simply to save face. To change would mean rethinking long-held doctrines, rewriting textbooks, and conceding the battle to the theists. It would mean respected educators had committed their careers to believing and teaching an error.

According to Dr. Phillip Johnson, "The theory is also protected by its cultural importance. It is the officially sanctioned creation story of modern society, and publicly funded educational authorities spare no effort to persuade the public to believe in it." Johnson went on to say that the dogmatism asserted by the scientific community over evolution relegated to the "lunatic fringe" all scientists who did not toe the evolutionary line. "Under the circumstances, prudent paleontologists understandably swallowed their doubts and supported the ruling ideology. To abandon the paradigm would be to abandon the scientific community."[27] This would mean losing out on research grant money, tenured professorships, and opportunities to publish.

It seems that the scientific community shows little tolerance for deviation from the basic principles of evolution, perhaps because the theory is too fragile to withstand it. Lockstep agreement is required to keep Charlie's hotel from collapsing into rubble.

It appears, however, that there is one even more basic reason that drives naturalists to cling to evolution: it gives them an alternative to God. As biologist Richard Dawkins writes, "Darwin made it possible to be an intellectually fulfilled atheist."[28]

It's a bit odd that so many modern scientists find God repugnant when almost all the founders of modern science were overtly Christian. The list includes Copernicus, Galileo, Boyle, Newton, Faraday, Pasteur, Maxwell, Mendel, Volta, Pascal, Kelvin, Morse, and many others.[29] These scientists did not see belief in God as antiscientific. On the contrary, their faith stabilized their confidence in science, enabling them to explore nature with confidence that the result would be orderly and would accord with reality.

Today, however, the ground has shifted. The dominant philosophy of the scientific world is naturalism, which is now the secularists' creed because it excludes from the universe any trace of divine influence. They hold to evolution because it is their only prop for the universe they want—a universe without God. Or perhaps more to the point, a universe where science is god.

In Their Own Words

How do we know this to be what modern evolutionists think? Can we read their minds or their hearts? No, but we can read their words. Throughout the decades of Darwinism's growing dominance, many prominent evolutionists in moments of candor have admitted explicitly that they cling to evolution despite its irrationalities because it gives them an alternative to God. Let's look at some examples.

Professor D. M. S. Watson of the University of London wrote, "[Evolution is] a theory universally accepted not because it can be proved by logically coherent evidence to be true but because the only alternative, special creation, is clearly incredible."[30] Dr. Watson's statement was a bold admission that his belief in evolution was not scientific; it was philosophical. He knew evolution to be scientifically insupportable, yet he adopted it because it gave him an alternative to belief in God.

Harvard biology professor and Nobel Prize winner George Wald believed the only reasonable explanation for the origin of life was spontaneous generation (by which he meant abiogenesis) because, as he put it, "The only alternative [is] to believe in a single, primary act of supernatural creation."[31] Wald maintained that although spontaneous generation is considered impossible, it must have happened because we are here, and he refused to consider creation by God as an option.[32]

In interviewing Richard Dawkins in 2008, Ben Stein asked, "What do you think is the possibility that intelligent design might turn out to be the answer to some issues in genetics or evolution?" Dawkins responded, "It could be that at some earlier time, somewhere in the universe, a civilization evolved by probably some kind of Darwinian means to a very, very high level of technology—and designed a form of life that they seeded onto perhaps this planet. . . . If you look at the details of biochemistry, molecular biology, you might find a signature of some sort of designer."

Since Dawkins admitted to the possibility of finding evidence of some kind of designer, Stein asked if that designer could possibly be God. Dawkins firmly insisted that it could not, saying, "No, nothing like that." As Stein noted later, "So Professor Dawkins was not against intelligent design, just certain types of designers, such as God."[33]

"I want atheism to be true," said New York University

philosophy professor Thomas Nagel, "and am made uneasy by the fact that some of the most intelligent and well-informed people I know are religious believers. It isn't just that I don't believe in God and, naturally, hope that I'm right in my belief. It's that I hope there is no God! I don't want there to be a God; I don't want the universe to be like that."[34]

Prominent geneticist Richard Lewontin, writing in the *New York Review of Books*, said:

> We take the side of science in spite of the patent absurdity of some of its constructs . . . in spite of the tolerance of the scientific community for unsubstantiated just-so stories, because we have a prior commitment, a commitment to materialism. . . . We are forced by our a priori adherence to material causes to create an apparatus of investigation and a set of concepts that produce material explanations, no matter how counter-intuitive, no matter how mystifying to the uninitiated. Moreover, that materialism is an absolute, for we cannot allow a Divine Foot in the door.[35]

Despite the lack of evidence for evolution, despite the natural laws that defy it, and despite its irrationalities and inconsistencies, these naturalists assert that the theory simply must be true because it is their only alternative to God. It appears that they find the idea of his authority over human life intolerable. In evolution they find an alternative with no supernatural strings attached. If we rose from lower animals, we have no responsibility to a higher power. Aldous Huxley, author of the classic *Brave New World*, admitted that he and many of his contemporaries were atheists because they wanted "liberation from a certain system of morality. We objected to the morality because it interfered with our sexual freedom."[36] As Huxley and the quotes above demonstrate, a universe without a deity is so important to naturalists that they are willing to sacrifice reason to maintain the illusion of evolution.

Phillip Johnson explained this pervasive Darwinian mindset, saying, "To scientific naturalists the notion that there could be a reality outside science is literally unthinkable." Their entrenched dogmatism enables them to reject God, creation, and all evidence that might discredit evolution, declaring it to be "a logically self-evident proposition requiring no empirical confirmation." This leaves Darwinism as nothing more than a mere tautology: "Naturalistic evolution is the only conceivable explanation for life, and so the fact that life exists proves it to be true."[37]

By supporting evolution and shutting out rational alternatives, naturalistic scientists may save face with their peers and keep their reputations intact today. But when the theory collapses in the future, as it inevitably will, history will lump evolutionists with those who believed in a flat earth and alchemy. As Malcolm Muggeridge, British philosopher and editor of *Punch*, asserted, "the theory of evolution . . . will be one of the great jokes in the history books of the future. Posterity will marvel that so very flimsy and dubious an hypothesis could be accepted with the incredible credulity that it has."[38]

It's highly likely that Muggeridge has accurately predicted evolution's future. The theory is already crumbling. For now, it survives largely because its proponents have banded together and defended it by expelling all residents of Darwin's hotel who will not agree to prop up its tottering walls.

Defending the Indefensible

You may think we must have grossly overstated the irrationalities of evolution. Surely if the theory is as unscientific and irrational as we have portrayed it, it would not be so widely accepted. Isn't it presumptuous for laymen to challenge a doctrine so widely recognized as one of the foundations of modern thought?

We certainly must avoid unthinking dogmatism in areas where we have no expertise. Yet we must not pretend that the naked emperor is wearing a suit. We must resist being intimidated by experts with an agenda—experts whose claims clash with established science, simple reason, and observable reality.

History shows that prevailing opinion often conflicts with

truth. When an idea becomes popular, it tends to gather momentum and run roughshod over reason. It seems to generate protective antibodies that attack all independent thought that challenges it. Differing viewpoints are repelled with hostility. Opposition invites the scorn of peers and the censure of the politically correct. Public conditioning becomes so pervasive that truth can no longer penetrate the preconceptions of the masses.

For example, before the discoveries of astronomer Nicolaus Copernicus (1473-1543), all Western universities taught *geocentrism*—that the universe revolves around the earth. Though Copernicus clearly showed this theory to be false, seventy-three years after his death the church placed his writings in the index of prohibited books, where it remained for one hundred forty-three years. His heliocentric theory countered the prevailing view that the earth was the center of the universe.

We hope you are reading this book because you would rather follow the truth than follow the crowd. The next time you encounter an evolutionist's explanation of any part of the theory, we urge you to put on your critical hat and examine the claim carefully. Was it backed up by empirical facts verified by experiment, tests, replication, or direct observation? Or was it merely a just-so story? When you find that it is just a story, we hope you will have the courage to resist the downstream pull of massive peer pressure to conform. Swimming upstream can be difficult, but it can also be exhilarating.

QUESTIONS FOR THOUGHT AND DISCUSSION

1. Why do you think Darwin's theory of evolution became the pervasive belief of secularism?

2. What is the difference between microevolution and macroevolution? Is either a valid truth?

3. Why should evolution be labeled a theory and not a fact of science?

4. Why can't the laws of nature explain origins?

5. How does irreducible complexity demonstrate creation over evolution?

6. How does the transition from reproduction by mitosis to sexual reproduction undermine the validity of evolution?

7. Why do most of today's scientists and influential institutions support evolution? How has the pressure of culture impacted your own views on evolution?

8

REASON'S EXILED ALLY

*How the exclusion of faith distorts
the search for authentic truth*

As a child you very likely spent many a summer night lying on the lawn and gazing into the star-saturated vastness of deep space. You located the North Star, the Big Dipper, and the gossamer haze of the Milky Way, and you identified various constellations and planets against a backdrop of countless celestial bodies.

As you stared into the heavens, a sense of awe began to engulf you. You pondered the fact that all the stars and planets within your range of vision are located within our own galaxy, the Milky Way—one hundred thousand light years in diameter—and our galaxy is only one among billions flung throughout deep space. You began to feel small as it dawned on you that our home planet is only a speck in a vast universe extending in all directions without end.

Without end! The concept of endlessness invaded your mind and stumped your powers of reason. As you pondered the idea, the gears in your brain began to grind and strain, grappling with realities beyond your capacity even to imagine. Surely nothing can stretch on and on into infinity without ending somewhere.

Yet when your childhood imagination tried to conceive of a limit to space—maybe it ended at an enormous wall or a gigantic glass bubble—you then faced the question of what exists beyond that bubble. Inevitably, more space extending—what word could describe it?—forever. You used a time-related word to express an impossible but inevitable spatial reality. Space has to extend forever, or infinitely, even though the concept of infinity seems impossible.

As you grew older and wiser, you still found it impossible for your imagination to grasp the inevitable infinitude of space. We humans cannot cope with the concept of space with or without limits. The impossible yet inevitable concept of infinity is simply more than our minds can digest.

Thinking about time presents the same dilemma. We cannot conceive of a beginning or an end of time because the only thing we can imagine prior to or beyond time is more time. The concept of anything existing without beginning or end is incomprehensible to us.

You did not realize it then, but in your common childhood musings, you were bumping up against the limits of reason, something that Enlightenment philosophers failed to take into account. The two dominant philosophies of the

Enlightenment—the philosophic, political, and scientific movement arising in the eighteenth century—were *rationalism* and *empiricism*. Enlightenment thinkers asserted that truth could be discovered either by sheer reason or by scientific investigation of the physical world. As a result, reason and science became supreme, and most of the philosophic and religious ideals of previous eras were cast aside.

We too believe in the power of reason to lead us toward truth, as we explained in considerable detail in chapter 4. Unlike the Enlightenment philosophers, however, we realize that reason has limitations, as you yourself must have begun to understand in those evenings under the stars.

The Limits of Reason

When we grapple with concepts such as endlessness and the origins of existence, we find ourselves at an impasse beyond which human comprehension cannot go. Reason simply cannot live up to the Enlightenment claims that it possesses the key to all knowledge. Reason cannot explain origins because, according to reason, everything that exists must be caused, which means—though it's hard to state in a noncontradictory way—that something had to exist prior to anything existing in order to cause existence. This forces us to the unfathomable conclusion that standing behind all causes there must be an ultimate *first cause* that is uncaused and self-existent.

The mind cannot encompass the idea that anything could exist without a beginning, which is the dilemma we face when contemplating both the naturalistic and the theistic explanations of origins. The big bang does not explain the origins of matter because it fails to explain the origin of the original singularity or the energy that set off its expansion. The matter and energy were either caused by some preexisting agent, or they were self-existent, or they came into existence out of nothing. Any of these alternatives make the big bang just as opaque to reason as the concept of God.

The rational mind cannot come to terms with the concept of lifeless, self-existent matter spontaneously generating life, reason, goodness, beauty, and meaning. Nor can it explain the alternative—a self-existent God who by acts of will brought all nature into being. Yet one of these alternatives must be true because existence cannot be explained apart from self-existence. Either matter and energy are self-existent or God is self-existent. Neither alternative is "possible" according to reason. Nothing can be self-existent, and nothing can be self-generating.

What should we do when faced with such alternatives that defy rational explanation? Should we flip a coin between naturalism and theism, or should we just throw up our hands at the whole question and walk away into agnosticism?

The Rational Step beyond Reason

The first principle we must observe is that it is not necessary for reason to comprehend a concept before it affirms it as true. For example, I (Tom) enjoy watching magic acts in which the illusionist performs feats that to my mind seem utterly impossible—levitation, sawing an assistant in half, making people disappear, plucking doves from the air, or even changing the color of a scarf from red to blue. I'm sure you've marveled at these tricks too. They appear to be performed by real magic that suspends or defies natural laws. I cannot comprehend how these illusions can be achieved by mere sleight of hand or visual deception. Yet despite my lack of understanding, I believe they are just that—illusions—and not the real, nature-defying magic they appear to be. I believe this, not because of what my senses tell me, but because I have a friend who is an illusionist, and he assures me that every performer's trick, no matter how seemingly impossible, is an illusion. My friend has always been honest and trustworthy, so I do not hesitate to believe that what he says is true despite the failure of my mind to comprehend it.

By a similar process, when weighing concepts beyond human understanding such as origins and endlessness, we cannot reach truth through reason alone. Whatever we discover to be the source of everything, we must believe it to be true despite the failure of reason to comprehend it. This means we must step beyond rational comprehension into uncharted territory. Necessity pushes us into that trackless region where we must be guided by a thing that most rationalists, secularists, and naturalists regard with lip-curling contempt—faith.

We know that the word *faith* grates on secularists' ears like fingernails on galvanized metal. It is another concept that naturalists have discarded as having no place in the mental furniture of a reasonable person. The secular assertion that rational thinkers rely on reason while religious believers rely on faith is another secular myth that needs to be confronted. In today's world of dominant rationalism, most people have been led to think of faith as reason's opposite, but that is largely because the true meaning of the word has been distorted. Today faith is most often characterized as a dogged, unthinking commitment to a belief unsupported by evidence or even to a belief that is discredited and irrational.

Valid faith is nothing like that. We should never exercise faith *in spite of* reason and evidence but always *because of* reason and evidence. Valid faith does not leap unguided into the dark; it moves only in the direction that reason points. When reason tallies the evidence and by rational necessity posits what the mind cannot comprehend, faith steps up and carries what reason postulates toward its logical conclusion. Reason directs; faith acts. Faith is the beam from the searchlight of reason. It pierces the darkness where reason points and illuminates the conclusion that reason postulates. Faith trusts what reason cannot see but knows must be true. When reason reaches the chasm it cannot cross, it identifies the bridge that faith must traverse. Reason leads to the altar; faith says, "I do." As Biola University philosophy professor J. P. Moreland put it, faith is "a trust in what we have reason to believe is true."[1]

Faith and reason are far from being opposites. In fact, they are allies. Faith is essentially blind without reason, and reason is sterile and powerless without faith. Blind faith undirected by reason is neither credible nor admirable. It is a foolish leap into the dark with no assurance of landing on the solid ground of truth. Faith is the rationally necessary step beyond comprehension into belief—a step regularly exercised by naturalists as well as theists. Faith is the passport into the uncharted territory of origins that lies beyond the borders of mental comprehension—territory inaccessible by reason to both naturalists and theists.

This means the choice between God and naturalism is not a choice between faith and reason. It is simply inaccurate to claim that naturalists reach their conclusions by reason and theists reach theirs by faith. Both naturalists and theists employ reason in evaluating evidence and analyzing probabilities to support their beliefs. When they encounter the question of origins, both find that reason reaches its inevitable impasse, which we described earlier. The naturalistic option for the source of matter, life, and order is just as mentally inconceivable as the theistic option. At this impasse, both naturalists and theists employ faith to step out into belief. In choosing God, theists take a step beyond reason into faith. In choosing naturalism, naturalists take a step beyond reason into faith. Neither alternative can be encompassed by reason, and neither is provable by empirical evidence. Only that step of faith will lead one to belief in either conclusion.

This does not mean, however, that the two conclusions are equally valid or that both conform to reality. And it certainly does not mean that both the rationalists and the theists have found their "own truth" that differs from other truths. These two opposing positions cannot both be objectively true. The true one, while lacking empirical proof, will have the full support of reason and evidence. The other will require a blind, undirected leap into the dark. The choice between God and naturalism boils down to what informs our faith. It can be informed by objective reason or it can be blinded by a skewed philosophy that throws reason off course. Our task is to decide which choice merits our faith by having the full support of reason.

To make this decision, we must compare the alternatives and determine which aligns best with the reality we experience. Which is the most consistent, and which is flawed by contradictions? Which squares with what our minds tell us must be true, and which requires that we deny what seems to be true in favor of an alternative narrative? Which best explains the existence of such phenomena as life, reason, thought, morality, love, meaning, and beauty?

The Naturalistic Resistance to Faith

Dr. Phil Zuckerman, writing in *Psychology Today*, asserts that faith has no part in the decisions of a true rationalist. Where the options are unverifiable, he says we should not employ faith; we should simply refrain from making choices. He rejects theism, claiming a lack of evidence, and maintains atheism as a default position:

Since you can't provide rational, evidence-based answers to such questions, I don't accept your theory or argument or belief or faith that everything was created by God. And in my skeptical rejection of your theological answer, I do not have faith in something else. I'm just humble and honest enough to accept my ignorance, and accept that the origin of creation remains a deep mystery.

Many people say that it takes faith to be an atheist. No, it does not. Atheism is simply the lack of a belief in a god. And as for who or what created the universe, we atheists say: who knows? That is not faith. That is an admission of ignorance.[2]

On the surface, Dr. Zuckerman's position seems reasonable, honest, and even humble. His claim to accept the origin of everything as "a deep mystery" seems to support his claim that his atheism requires no faith. He believes in nothing. If he is being honest with us, his determination to maintain ignorance as to the source of creation must necessarily mean he not only rejects theism but naturalism as well. Naturalism makes its own claims about origins, which must also be taken on faith.

First, we will point out that if Dr. Zuckerman is truly neutral about his endorsement of any theory of origins, he should call himself an agnostic rather than an atheist. But let's not quibble about semantics. The fact is, Dr. Zuckerman is not neutral in his belief. He unequivocally endorses secularism, having written several books defending it. In his writings he consistently presents secularism as a worldview freed from the influence of theism. In his book *What It Means to Be Moral*, he debunks theism and endorses what he calls "seven secular virtues."[3] In another *Psychology Today* article defining secularism, Zuckerman writes, "To be secular is to maintain a naturalistic worldview."[4] With this statement, he makes it even clearer that he is not neutral. Like all the atheists we encounter, as exemplified by those quoted in the previous chapter, in rejecting theism, Zuckerman has chosen naturalism as his alternative. This means faith has slipped into his thinking. Belief in naturalism requires faith just as does belief in God. It is not a neutral position, and belief in it requires faith-based assumptions. Dr. Zuckerman has actually made a faith choice between alternatives, which he has tried to disguise as neutrality.

Suppose Dr. Zuckerman had been true to his claim of maintaining complete neutrality between God and naturalism, which would mean he refrained from endorsing either option. This stance may have been "humble and honest" as he claimed, but we do not consider it to be admirable. To deliberately remain in willful ignorance when facing the most important question one will ever encounter does not seem a reasonable response. He may be different from most atheists, but almost always when one chooses ignorance—as Zuckerman claimed to do—then something other than neutrality is involved. Usually, it can be expressed in the words of Professor Thomas Nagel, whom we quoted in the previous chapter: "I don't want there to be a God; I don't want the universe to be like that."[5]

G. K. Chesterton pinpointed the absurdity of considering it a mark of superior intellect for one to have an "open mind" that refuses to come to conclusions when he said, "The object of opening the mind, as of opening the mouth, is to shut it again on something solid."[6]

We are convinced that Dr. Zuckerman is mistaken in saying belief in God is theological and not rational or evidence-based. As we and many other writers have amply demonstrated—thinkers such as C. S. Lewis, J. P. Moreland, G. K. Chesterton, Stephen C. Myer, and William Lane Craig—theism is supported by powerful and rational evidence that every skeptic, atheist, or agnostic should seriously consider.

To all these difficulties that arise with Dr. Zuckerman's statement, we must add one more. He says atheism does not require faith; it simply accepts ignorance. This is not true. Willful atheism that sidesteps life's most important question by declining to pursue evidence to a conclusion does indeed display faith—faith in the capacity of one's own mind to decide that truth is not of vital importance. When we do this, we essentially make ourselves our own god.

Atheism that refuses to dig for answers and simply leaves the question on the table while getting on with life is the easy way out. It merely kicks the can on down the road to be dealt with later when life's inevitable challenges make questions of meaning and purpose more acute. We hope you agree that it is better to do our digging now so we will be prepared when those challenges hit us.

Naturalism or Theism: Which Merits Faith?

As we have repeatedly noted in this book, naturalism's explanations of origins fail to address the central issue. The big bang fails to explain how matter and energy came to be. It passes over the ultimate questions of what brought that dense point of matter into existence and what triggered its sudden expansion. Abiogenesis merely asserts that life arose from nonliving matter but fails to provide any evidence whatsoever that this has ever occurred or could occur. It also fails to explain how or why a megacomplex cell receptive to life and capable of performing all the functions of life was formed before life existed. Evolution claims that life diversified into multiple species, but it fails to provide evidence other than just-so stories that violate incontrovertible laws of nature.

Naturalism gives us a universe filled with contradictions and illusions. It gives us creatures that seem to have been designed but were not, laws that are known to be inviolable but were violated, morality that seems to have authority but does not, reason that seems to be rational despite its non-rational origins, realities that seem to be true but are false, and beauty that seems to have meaning but does not. To naturalists, all these "seemings" are illusory. They cannot be sure that any are real. Despite the appearance of order and meaning that emanates from all that exists, naturalists must force themselves to believe that beneath the surface, all existence is senseless, mechanistic, meaningless, and purposeless. They have no rational alternative, for to remain naturalists, they must deny the presence of any living, supernatural, purposeful first cause that could give meaning and purpose to existence.

Now let's look at the theistic alternative. Nothing about the concept of God as creator violates evidence, reason, or any branch of science. Reason tells us that the existence of the universe demands a self-existent first cause; theism posits God as the self-existent first cause. Science and reason tell us that no effect can be greater than its cause; theism tells us that God who is greater than the universe caused it to be. History and experience tell us that morality is universal, which is best explained by its being God-implanted within the human conscience. Science tells us that life comes only from life; creation tells us that life resides eternally in God, and he imparted it to his creation. Science tells us that nature runs down and dissipates, which squares with the biblical narrative asserting that God made everything originally perfect, but it incurred damage and began to degenerate. (We will look at this more closely in chapter 11.)

Nothing less than God meets all the requirements. The case for God is that simple. We believers see him as the only possible answer to life and existence that fits into place without jarring the order of the universe or insulting the consistency of science (as we have shown that naturalism does). God's existence cannot be proved by scientific evidence, for science is limited to nature and cannot probe into an extra-natural realm. Yet when considering the source of origins, reason tells us that an extranatural realm must exist. The concept of God is not in opposition to reason; it is simply above reason. It is not irrational; it is superrational. Though reason cannot comprehend God, it can safely postulate God as a rational necessity to account for the reality we experience. Faith can safely step out on that certainty.

God must be the absolute that undergirds all reality, or all reality is inexplicable, meaningless, and riddled with contradictions. We might get by with a claim of some natural prime mover other than God in a dark, dead world where nothing but cold, inert matter existed, but not in this world pulsating with life, energy, meaning, delight, love, and beauty. Such things are beyond the capacity of mere nature to provide. The existence of these realities gives us assurance that an intelligent, creative, and powerful being exists in much the same way we know that subatomic particles exist. Subatomic particles are invisible and beyond the reach of present scientific instrumentation, but we can infer their existence by observing effects on atoms that only something like subatomic particles could cause. God is invisible, but we can infer his existence by noting effects observable in the universe that only something like a god could cause. When reason tallies up the evidence, it points to an intelligent, self-existent being out there beyond the reach of comprehension. But not beyond the reach of the combined arms of reason and faith.

Expanding Our Horizons

Edwin A. Abbott's novel *Flatland* is populated with two-dimensional geometric creatures living in a flat, two-dimensional world consisting only of length and width.[7] These beings have no height at all. They cannot conceive of the third dimension of height because it is outside their experience and their mode of existence. Yet as one of them discovers by reason, a third dimension could and probably does exist, though his limited experience in two dimensions renders him unable to imagine the configuration of it.

Like the flatlanders, we who exist in the world of nature, where everything has a beginning and an end, cannot conceive of a supernatural dimension where a being exists who has no beginning or end. We can, however, rationally postulate that such a dimension must exist in order to explain existence in our own dimension. It is not necessary to understand a truth before recognizing that it must be true.

When we insist on complete understanding before we believe, we make our minds our gods. We trust our minds to be the ultimate judge of all things. We rely on our intelligence and understanding as our ultimate absolute. But the human mind makes a poor absolute. Not only does it shut down in the face of the great cosmic questions of origins and endlessness, it stumbles daily over ordinary things, as we're sure you've noticed. You've undoubtedly misfigured your checkbook or misplaced your car keys. Maybe you've been stumped by the *New York Times* crossword puzzle or by IRS tax forms. Or you've forgotten anniversaries, birthdays, and names. Minds like ours do not have what it takes to be our own gods or to comprehend the mode of existence of a supernatural God. In fact, a god we could comprehend would not be a god worth having.

To find the ultimate truth that gives meaning to our lives, we must not close ourselves inside the borders of our minds. We must find the courage to venture out past what we can fully understand. We cannot understand how it's possible for an uncaused first cause to exist, but we can understand that without a self-existent first cause, existence itself is impossible. This is why theists are convinced that God exists. He is a rational necessity.

If a supernatural realm outside and above nature does exist, we should not expect to understand it clearly. Anthropologist Loren Eiseley wrote of deliberately touching a pencil to the giant web of an orb spider. As he reflected on the spider's reaction, he realized that her web was her entire world. The spider had neither knowledge of him nor the ability to comprehend that there existed an outside, superior power that could so invade her world.[8] The spider's limited senses made it impossible for her to comprehend him, while he could study her at will. The higher can understand the lower, but not vice versa.

Confined as we are to the web of nature, why should we think it impossible that our universe may be contained within a larger realm of supernature that is beyond the capacity of our senses? Should flatlanders deny a third dimension merely because they cannot imagine it? As Plato postulated in his famous shadows-in-a-cave allegory, when we imagine a spirit world, we think of it as insubstantial and ethereal. But if such a world exists, as he believed it did, it would likely be even more substantial and solid than our own. This universe of ours may be a mere shadowy reflection of a greater reality beyond it. Our failure to comprehend the supernatural gives us no reason to deny its existence.

We can understand how a secularist saturated in naturalism from childhood would resist buying into the supernaturalism we are describing. Nothing about God fits neatly into the secular world's naturalistic box. He seems out of place—an anachronism like a horse-drawn buggy in a Lexus showroom or an abacus in an Apple computer store. The ancient God of the Bible seems out of step with everything about our secular culture. Belief in him has largely become an embarrassment in today's media, entertainment, and education, as well as in a growing number of work and social environments.

No doubt, part of the modern secularist's discomfort with God stems from the frank accounts of miracles and supernaturalism that fill the Bible. When read through the lens of our modern sensibilities, the stories of creation, Adam and Eve, Noah and the Flood, the tower of Babel, and Daniel in the lions' den have the flavor of myth. The feel of these stories stands in sharp contrast to encyclopedic explanations of the big bang, evolution, and DNA. The secular mind is steeped so thoroughly in the mechanics and language of science that it tends to dismiss biblical texts as outdated relics from humanity's naive past.

Because God is such an embarrassment to twenty-first-century secularists, many have simply willed him out of existence. To avoid the discomfort of being out of step with our sophisticated culture, they close their eyes to the possibility that he exists.

Despite this anachronistic discomfort and embarrassing supernaturalism, what if God really does exist? Despite Thomas Nagel's wish—"I don't want the world to be like that!"—what if the world *is* like that? If God does exist, then he is the central reality of the universe. It makes no sense to close our eyes to his existence merely because we find it unpalatable or because he has set up some aspect of reality contrary to the way we would have it. If God does exist, that monumental fact must be faced squarely.

We must be wary of unfounded, closed-minded claims about reality like that of the late astronomer Carl Sagan who stated, "The cosmos is all that is or ever was or ever will be."[9] There is no way for any naturalist to know this—no way to know that the universe described by science is all that exists. It's like the orb spider claiming there is no world outside its web or the flatlander asserting that no third dimension is possible. It is an assertion made in ignorance—an unfounded claim based solely on one's own experience or philosophy or on an overconfidence in the supremacy of naturalism.

Sagan's entrenched dogmatism against the possibility of the supernatural is not merely unwarranted arrogance; it is dangerous. If the supernatural realm does exist, other claims made by theists may be true as well. Theists insist that this

God who exists by logical necessity created us for a purpose, and we have a duty to find that purpose by learning more about him and what he expects of his creation. Let's not forget that he also promises endless life filled with immense joy and meaning to those who follow the faith that leads to him. We hope that you yourself will experience this promise. To miss out on it is the greatest tragedy that can befall anyone.

QUESTIONS FOR THOUGHT AND DISCUSSION

1. Why do we find it impossible to comprehend self-existence and endlessness?

2. Is atheism a faith? What about naturalism? What about Christianity?

3. Is creation a more rational explanation for origins than the big bang? Why or why not?

4. What is the authentic relationship between faith and reason?

5. What is the nature of true faith?

6. What do we mean by the term "rational necessity"?

7. How should those who believe in God handle unanswered questions, missing evidences, and gnawing doubts in light of their step of faith toward him?

PART THREE

RAISING THE CURTAIN ON TRANSCENDENCE

9

THE UNQUENCHABLE
DESIRE FOR CAMELOT

*Are meaning and fulfillment possible in
a universe closed off from transcendence?*

In the celebrated legend of King Arthur, we read of a man endowed with great abilities, great dreams, and great promise. Perhaps you have read the story or seen one of the many movies based on it. In T. H. White's telling of the story, *The Once and Future King*, Arthur begins life as a humble servant in the manor of a baron. As a teenager, he is elevated to the throne of Britain when he draws the sword Excalibur from solid stone—a feat that mature men of power and ambition had been unable to accomplish.

With the aid of the wizard Merlyn, young King Arthur begins his reign intent on infusing his court with the lofty ideals of purity, justice, equality, and chivalry. His reputation spreads, and he builds the magnificent castle on the legendary site known as Camelot. Soon his ideals and successes draw noblemen from throughout Britain and beyond, who place themselves in his service as knights. He installs a massive, round table in the great hall of Camelot, around which he seats his knights to emphasize their equality with each other.

All goes well with Arthur's court. He rules justly, and his knights enforce peace, lift the fallen, rescue the oppressed, and uphold positive ideals in all their activities. The kingdom prospers.

The seeds of doom, however, have already been planted. Arthur's most noble and trusted knight, Sir Lancelot, engages in an affair with his queen. A vengeful son, the product of an adulterous affair in Arthur's past, shows up to sow discord. These seeds sprout tentacles that slowly work their way through Arthur's court and finally pull it down when a war of rebellion brings about Arthur's death and the collapse of Camelot.

The saga of Arthur and Camelot has maintained a place in our literature for centuries, partly because it has all the elements of a good story: magic, romance, adventure, intrigue. But on another level, readers may also recognize and relate to the rise-and-fall rhythm of life. The tale is a perfect metaphor for the tragic story of the world as seen through the eyes of naturalists. In their view, we humans have advanced from our humble beginnings as single-celled, mud-dwelling organisms through several intermediate animal stages to become the glorious, thinking beings we are today. Throughout history we have created great civilizations, each more advanced than the previous in terms of wealth, fame, order, and power. We in the twenty-first century are convinced we have progressed

JOSH McDOWELL AND THOMAS WILLIAMS

far beyond the accomplishments of all previous cultures. The inventions and amassed knowledge that lift us above our ancestors are testaments to the capacity of humans to improve almost infinitely. Our harnessing of electric and fossil-fuel power, mass manufacturing, rapid transportation, instant communication, electronic technology, medical marvels, and space exploration give evidence to our conviction that we possess superior genius. When we look at the dreams and plans now on the drawing board, we feel assured of a future filled with glories even more magnificent.

Even as we exult in our accomplishments, the law of entropy gnaws away like a burrowing worm, eroding order, dissipating matter, and burning irreplaceable energy. The sun is slowly consuming itself and will burn out and die in a few billion years, as will all suns in all galaxies. The earth will end much sooner as the dying sun expands and boils off the earth's water. Stephen Hawking was even more pessimistic, predicting that the earth probably has less than a thousand years before a combination of natural and human forces make it uninhabitable.[1] Entropy will leave the naturalist's universe cold and void, with all humanity's accomplishments dead and forgotten.

How is it possible to find meaning in a universe where everything that exists is moving inexorably toward oblivion—where no human accomplishment, however grand and imposing, will endure? When God is removed from the universe, not only is the possibility of human immortality lost, the possibility of finding real meaning in anything is lost as well because everything—including us—is doomed to end in nothingness. Without God, we are alone and unprotected in a dying universe without plan or purpose. We may try to find momentary comfort in the theory of evolution, which posits that people are gradually improving and may eventually overcome the deficiencies in their own nature and even conquer death. Yet the hard truth is that the universe is running down, and nothing can be done to stop it. In the mind of the naturalist, the story will end in the tragedy of Camelot—the castle in rubble, the Round Table splintered, the king dead, the bodies of the brave knights strewn across the battlefield, and all ideals reduced to ashes.

Nothing More than a Ripple?

Because this predicted end of the naturalist's world is a thousand or more years away, you may think it is much too distant to negate the value of your present accomplishments. But if the naturalistic model is correct, you will enter that ultimate and permanent oblivion within a few decades. Think about it: within the next ten or so decades, everyone presently alive on the planet will be dead. If naturalism is correct, that death is final. It will be as if none of these lives ever existed, and nothing they accomplished—even if it's a cure for cancer or the common cold—will have any lasting effect or meaning.

If you happen not to believe God exists, there is little point in gazing into the stars and asking why you have been placed on this planet because without God there is no being in the endless, black silence even to hear the question.

Without God there can be no *why*—no explanation, ratio-nale, or meaning for existence.

The well-known Jewish Rabbi Harold Kushner tells of a distressed man who came to him for counseling. The man explained that two weeks prior, for the first time in his life, he had attended the funeral of a coworker his own age. The friend had died suddenly and unexpectedly, and as the man explained to Rabbi Kushner, he could not get the death out of his mind. He and his coworkers were thinking it could just as easily have been them. He said, "They have already replaced him at the office. . . . Two weeks ago, he was working fifty feet away from me and now it's as if he never existed. It's like a rock falling into the pool of water and then the water is the same as it was before but the rock isn't there anymore." He went on to explain that he had slept little since his friend's death. "I just can't stop thinking that it could have happened to me, and a few days later I would be forgotten as if I never lived. Shouldn't a man's life be more than that?"[2]

The cold face of death awakened this poor man to the fact that without something to give human life transcendent value, his own life was nothing more than a momentary rip-ple in a placid pond that would absorb him as if he had never existed. A sense of meaning is critical to man's well-being. As psychiatrist Carl Jung said, "About a third of my cases are suffering from no clinically definable neurosis, but from the senselessness and emptiness of their lives. . . . This can well be described as the general neurosis of our time."[3]

During the COVID-19 pandemic, Gabe Scuderi,

a twenty-four-year employee in a New Jersey Lysol factory, came home to find his daughter waiting for him at the door. She greeted him as a hero. She had been watching news coverage and learned the vital role of Lysol spray in combating the spread of the disease. "It's the first time I felt this isn't only a job," Scuderi said. "We're on the front lines now."[4] Before that day, Scuderi's job was just a job, but now he saw that he was part of something bigger than himself. It gave his everyday work meaning and purpose.

We do not deny that work and what we accomplish for the good of society can and does give humans a sense of meaning. As Pope John Paul wrote, "Man expresses and fulfills himself by working," especially when his work contributes to "the common good." He goes on to say, however, that atheism removes ultimate meaning from work by denying the possibility of transcendent values.[5] What value can there be in our accomplishments if we and all beneficiaries of our work are to be snuffed out forever within the short span of eight or ten decades?

This principle applies to the whole of life. To find meaning, we must sense that our being and our endeavors have a purpose above ourselves. We must sense that we are part of something of lasting importance and infinite value.

A World without Meaning

Without God, humanity's existence is meaningless, and our future is hopeless. If we are not the products of a creator who made us for a purpose, we are merely robotic machines that emerged accidentally and have no reason for being. Nothing we do has ultimate meaning. We are programmed by random natural forces with reflexes and responses that cause us to do whatever we do automatically. Without God, freedom has no meaning, responsibility has no meaning, and goodness, heroism, justice, and love have no meaning. Neither do hate, lust, treachery, lying, or cowardice. If we are nothing more than randomly evolved machines, a person who commits murder is merely doing what a machine of a given type and programming is conditioned to do under a given set of circumstances and stimuli. In a world without God, people, their ideals, and all their activities are aimlessly produced and utterly meaningless.

In the universe of the naturalist, humankind is no different from anything else that exists. Each of us is merely an accidental and temporary cluster of atoms bearing no more importance than any other cluster. You have no more meaning than a rock, a fence post, a dog, or a cockroach. In the naturalist's world, we are nothing more than aimless lumps of matter stuck to the aimless mass of matter from which we came, floating in the empty void of a meaningless universe that will burn itself out as blindly as it banged itself in.

In an article on the beginning and end of the universe, Rick Gore, a senior writer for *National Geographic*, wrote, "So what is the point of a universe that ends in such oblivion? The more I begin to comprehend the universe, the more that question bothers me. I have no answer, beyond some memories that will not decay."[6] We can easily forgive Mr. Gore for tempering his despair with a little rhetorical wishful thinking, but we all know that if his view of the universe is correct, his memories *will* decay. The passing of the universe will leave nothing at all in its wake, not even a memory. To Mr. Gore and those who share his philosophy, the story of the universe is a cruel tragedy of matter jolting itself to life, waking itself to consciousness, raising itself to intelligence, and dreaming itself into eternity, only to face inevitable, unalterable, total oblivion. It is Camelot repeated.

It seems ironic that naturalists, pronouncing the realm of nature to be the sum total of reality, thought they were freeing themselves by getting rid of the oppressive idea of God. Instead they imprisoned themselves inside a dead-end universe with no way out. If God exists in a supernatural realm above nature, we have a doorway out of the doomed and boxed-in system of nature into an infinite realm without limits. Instead of enlarging humanity's universe, the naturalists' removal of God has shrunk it to the size of a coffin. Novelist John Updike put it plainly enough, "If this physical world is all, then it is a closed hell in which we are confined, as Pascal said elsewhere, like prisoners in chains, condemned to watch other prisoners being slain."[7]

Meaning simply cannot be found apart from God. Either God is the creator of the universe and has an eternal plan for it, or the universe is meaningless. Either God is the source of moral law, or morality is an illusion. Either God is the source of reason, or everything is irrational. It's as if naturalistic philosophies are sweeping us downstream through the rapids of a swift river, and we must choose between climbing onto a solid rock or plunging over a waterfall. One option offers security and a solid grip on stable reality; the other ends in a tumbling fall into a void where nothing has meaning and nothing is true. The choice is between God and nothing. We have no other alternatives.

We realize we have painted a pretty grim picture of the impossibility of finding meaning in a world without God. But we believe it to be an accurate picture. Young naturalists embarking on the voyage of life with high hopes and grand ambitions may not immediately feel these waves of despair. The freshness of each new experience may keep at bay the realization of how meaningless all activities are in a godless universe. As we noted in chapter 1, when this realization does hit them, they may accept it stoically as just the way things are and face the grim reality of meaninglessness with resigned acceptance and courage. On the other hand, they may try to escape despair by immersing themselves in pleasure, focusing on what feels good: gratifying all desires; filling empty days with wine, women, and song; letting repeated sensation compensate for the senselessness of existence.

This was the approach taken by English novelist Aldous Huxley, whom we quoted briefly in the previous chapter. He did not want the world to have meaning because he realized meaning would require the existence of God, and that would restrict his freedom to live as he wished. As he put it:

I had motives for not wanting the world to have meaning, consequently assumed it had none. . . . For myself, as no doubt for most of my contemporaries, the philosophy of meaninglessness was essentially an instrument of liberation. The liberation we desired was simultaneously liberation from a certain political and economic system and liberation from a certain system of morality. We objected to the morality because it interfered with our sexual freedom.[8]

Those who reject God to gain freedom don't realize that the existence of God gives them the only real freedom this universe offers. It frees them from the permanent imprisonment of death. It is more freedom than we can ever find on our own terms. Atheists fleeing from God are like captive animals running from the animal rescue agent who has entered the cage to free them. Atheists will remain imprisoned within themselves and their constricted universe until they allow God to open their lives to freedom.

George Sanders, a highly successful actor in the cinema's golden age, was a man who had everything the "good life" has to offer. He appeared in more than ninety films, won an Oscar, married four wives, had numerous affairs with Hollywood's most glamorous women, traveled at will, and made good money. Yet it was not enough to give his life meaning. At age sixty-five, Sanders took his own life at a seaside resort in Barcelona. He left a suicide note reading, "Dear World: I am leaving because I am bored. I feel I have lived long enough. I am leaving you with your worries in this sweet cesspool—good luck."[9]

None of naturalists' ways of coping with meaninglessness

has been found to work indefinitely. Stoicism is brave and admirable, but it's a mask, a false front hiding an inner despair. Hedonism eventually exhausts itself in repetition and becomes part of the meaninglessness one is trying to escape. Drink drowns reality only temporarily. Endless entertainment becomes a cycle of the same old, same old. Travel leaves one jaded with an "I've-seen-it-all" feeling. After a succession of sexual encounters, naturalists find that an endless stream of partners does not satisfy. It only mocks the desire for oneness with an exclusive mate—the foundational desire that underlies the sexual impulse. A truly meaningful purpose for living cannot be found in the world of naturalism.

The Reality of Meaning

The very fact that human beings desire meaning and feel a sense of bleakness without it tells us something. When we complain that our existence lacks meaning, we tacitly admit that meaning must exist. The fact that we have a concept of meaning demonstrates that whether or not we believe meaning actually exists, we can at least imagine its existence. This is telling because it is impossible to imagine anything that is completely foreign to our experience. The most creative human thinkers develop their concepts solely by discovering, reordering, and synthesizing elements collected through their senses and experiences. No one ever comes up with anything truly new and original. This tells us that since meaning can be imagined or thought of, it must exist as a reality.

Of course, we can claim to imagine things we have neither seen nor experienced—flying cows, grotesquely shaped
alien beings, or water flowing uphill. But such mental fabrications are inevitably assembled from the raw material
we have gathered from actual experience. Even a mind as
supremely creative as that of Albert Einstein, who postulated
a fourth dimension that included time and curved space, had
the raw materials of time and solid geometry to work with.
As someone has said, "If you steal from one source, it's called
plagiarism. If you steal from several sources, it's called creativity." Recombining or reshaping what we have experienced
through our senses defines the limit of what we can create
or even imagine. For example, try to imagine a new primary
color, a sixth sense, a fourth dimension, or a third sex that
is not a combination or extension of those that exist already.

The fact that we can imagine, comprehend, or even deny
the concept of meaning shows that meaning must be a reality. Otherwise, we could never have thought of it. It is impossible to complain of meaninglessness unless we have some
idea of what meaning should be. If light had never existed, it
would be impossible to imagine it, and we would not know
to complain of darkness. The idea of meaning is with us
because it is a reality, and we cannot escape the innate sense
of purpose that emanates from everything that exists.

Reality as described by naturalism cannot supply meaning. The reason, as we have already noted, is that naturalism
by definition claims that the natural universe is all that exists.
Since the naturalist believes the universe was born without

purpose and will die without purpose, it cannot provide ultimate meaning. Meaning must be rooted in purpose and the possibility of fulfilling that purpose.

According to theists, that is exactly what God provides. He created the universe to fulfill an eternal purpose, and he created humanity as his agents in fulfilling that purpose. We humans find meaning for our own lives when we discover how our individual purposes fit into his overarching purpose. There is no alternate source for meaning. It must be rooted outside the closed system of the naturalist's universe, which ultimately offers nothing but death and eternal oblivion. Only when we go outside the natural universe and tap into the realm of the supernatural where unending life and eternity are possible can we be assured of experiencing meaning.

The Beauty of Meaning

I (Tom) sat across the restaurant table from a highly educated former agnostic who had just crossed the border into full belief in God. Remembering my own conversion, I assumed that, like most of us, this man decided to become a Christian because of the beauty of creation or the promise of heaven or perhaps the threat of judgment. Or maybe like my colleague, Josh, he came to belief by exploring all the historical and rational evidences for God and Christianity. He insisted, however, that what led him to belief was none of these things.

"The thing that drew me to God," he explained, "was the sense of meaning and stability that having a God brings to the universe. It is something I had longed for all my life. I appreciate all the personal advantages that come with belief in God—a sense of groundedness and stability and the assurance of an unending life of joy. But I would have believed despite the promise of heaven or the threat of hell. I can see that without God, the universe has no possible meaning. Without God I was adrift in a sea of 'whys' that could never be answered. And that was becoming unbearable."

My friend was right. The simple fact of God's existence is enough to give anyone a strong sense of meaning. Just knowing that God exists bathes the universe with purpose and glory that vanishes when we see it as the product of blind chance. Yet the wonder of it all is that this God who created the universe loves his creation—not only as an overall accomplishment of his extravagant creativity; he loves each person he created as dearly and individually as an only child. When we turn to God, we gain assurance of meaning, not only in a theoretical sense but also in a direct and personal sense. The God of the universe has a plan for his creation that involves sharing eternity with us. Each of us is designed to fulfill a specific part of this purpose, and this invitation to a relational partnership with God is our ultimate source of meaning.

How God Provides Meaning

Today's secular culture places a high value on individualism and independence. That emphasis on self-sufficiency causes many people to shun belief in God because of Christianity's requirement of recognizing responsibility to a higher power. If you are not a believer, the idea of being forced into a box or called to march in lockstep to the beat of someone else's drum may repel you. You may fear that the application of Christianity's rules reduces everyone to cookie-cutter sameness. We regretfully admit that some Christians may find themselves in churches that indeed do try to impose unhealthy, legalistic rules on their members instead of freeing them to express their God-given uniqueness.

These impressions and expressions of Christianity are seriously mistaken. In fact, we are convinced that only Christianity enables you to become all you are created to be. At birth, each of us is instilled with natural inclinations and talents. Usually we discover these proclivities early, and we feel drawn to exercise and develop them. It's true, of course, that we can develop our talents into vocations with or without God. Generally, the difference is that without God, the talent will be turned inward so that its results will benefit the self. This is not universally true, for we know of many unbelievers whose talents have benefited humanity greatly. Even when people do not believe in God, they can find satisfaction in imitating his nature. But when one submits his talent to God, it will be expanded outward to benefit others—which ultimately will boomerang to benefit the self as well.

We are all as different from each other as tree leaves. We each have some aspect of talent and personality that no one else in world history has been given. We are given this one-of-a-kind specialness to reflect something of God's character in a way that no one else can. God encourages full development of this uniqueness to bring about its benefit to society and to those who believe in him. The Bible expresses this by comparing the church to a body, which needs all its varied parts—hands, feet, eyes, head, etc.—in order to function.

If you are not a believer—or even if you are—you may ask how being a Christian provides any more meaning to using your talents. The answer is that Christianity sees our present life as something like a training field for developing our natural abilities for their ultimate uses, which will come into play in the afterlife that fills eternity. God has a place for you in the eternal realm and a task or tasks that you were created to fulfill—tasks that will keep you active, creative, meaningfully employed, and growing in wisdom and abilities literally forever.

Forever is a very long time, and you may wonder how even eternity can provide unending meaning and fulfillment. Surely at some point, no matter how well you develop and exercise your talents, boredom from repetition is bound to set in. Surely you will eventually reach the limits of variety and newness, and routine will begin to sap all sense of meaning and fulfillment even from the most creative or exciting of tasks.

Be assured, eternity will not let you down. Far from being an extended existence of endless repetition, it will offer a vital experience of endless growth and development without limits. In his book *The Last Battle*, the final story in the Chronicles of Narnia, C. S. Lewis presents an image of heaven that we could characterize as the inversion of a Russian matryoshka doll. You've seen them—a set of five to seven or so carved wooden dolls of decreasing size, each fitting inside the other. As Lewis describes heaven in Narnia, it works in the opposite way. As one advances through eternity, each experience expands and becomes larger than the one before rather than smaller. New vistas, new dimensions, new experiences, new challenges, new joys open eternally, each previously unimagined and each more glorious than the one before. Meaning and fulfillment themselves become expanding eternal experiences.

One would think that with this offer of eternity dangling before them, people would flock to churches in droves. That's not happening because the secular system has always opposed the church, portraying it as a staid, humdrum, downer institution that frowns on joy. We must admit that some churches deserve this reputation. Many other churches have lost their appeal because of the way they have responded to secularism. They have tried to compete on secularism's terms, making the Christian life so easy that it seems insipid and almost as meaningless as secularism. Many churches have become theaters of entertainment, offering a watered-down, feel-good theology that requires little commitment and teaches mostly ways to improve one's immediate lifestyle, comfort, happiness, and sometimes even one's wealth. People easily see through this thin, watery religion, and what they see is that it seems to offer no more meaning than raw secularity.

Whether or not you are a believer, you are no doubt turned off by the way some churches have caved in to secularism and postmodernism. Even when we disagree with people, we respect them when they remain true to their beliefs and stand by their guns in defending them. We rightly expect churches to stand for unchangeable truths. But when they move with the times and compromise their principles in order to increase membership—adopting or endorsing practices their denominations have condemned for centuries—why should they expect culture to take them seriously? Or when they claim to stand for biblical morality but turn a blind eye when their pastors or priests commit adultery, embezzlement, or pedophilia, why should they be exempt from the culture's scorn?

The fact is, no one is perfect, and all institutions, whether religious or secular, have within them members whose motives are less than stellar. Churches are no exception. But a few hypocrites no more invalidate a church than a few cowards invalidate an army. A strong army remains functional and essential despite the presence of a few compromised soldiers. In virtually all churches there will be a mix of authentic Christians and nominal or even hypocritical Christians. Many who claim Christianity fail to live it. This is a shame the church has to bear, and we plead with you not to judge the Christian faith as a whole by those who are hypocritical or who represent it poorly.

Authentic Christianity is neither insipid nor easy. It offers a challenge and requires commitment and dedication. There is a cost. On January 10, 2022, the University of Georgia football team, the Bulldogs, won the NCAA national championship. Every player on that team had a unique talent for playing the game. Each developed that talent, usually from early childhood, by playing on Pop Warner and high school teams before heading for college. The young men ran for miles, and they worked out in gyms lifting weights to improve their strength and stamina. When they made the team, they endured grueling daily practices and learned their assigned moves in complex running and passing plays. The payoff came when they made the starting lineup and, finally, won the ultimate college football prize—the national championship.

To win this prize, the players had to submit to their coach. They were not their own; they belonged to a team and developed loyalty, responsibility, and love for their fellow teammates. Not a single player on the Bulldog team played football out of necessity. Not one was forced. All worked their tails off voluntarily because they found meaning and fulfillment in dedicating themselves to a cause bigger than themselves—a cause that utilized their skills, gave their efforts meaning in relationship to others, and gave them a way to accomplish a meaningful goal.

That is very much like what God offers you. Not an easy life with no bumps, but if you place yourself under his direction, a meaningful, fulfilling life with the greatest reward any human can imagine awaits at the end.

We are convinced that believing in God offers the only path to real meaning. We must believe in him to make sense out of existence. Nothing fits together as it should or has real meaning unless God is the ultimate reality behind it all. The universe takes on meaning only because God made it and has a plan for it. Your life takes on meaning because he created you for a particular eternal purpose, which you can find only in acknowledging his existence and coming into a proper relationship with him.

QUESTIONS FOR THOUGHT AND DISCUSSION

1. In a naturalistic universe, why are humans no more meaningful than bugs, weeds, rocks, or any other natural phenomena?

2. If human beings are accidental machines, can we rationally judge any person's actions to be good or evil? Why or why not?

3. Why is there no possible source of meaning in a completely naturalistic universe?

4. Why is the position of not believing in God at odds with reality?

5. Name some of humanity's attempts to find meaning. Why don't they work?

6. Is it possible to find meaning without dedication, effort, and relationships? Why or why not?

7. Do you agree with the argument in this chapter that God is the only ultimate source of meaning in the universe? Why or why not? What difference does your belief make in your life?

10

THE KEY TO REVELING IN BEAUTY AND JOY

What do sunsets, symphonies, and
sunflowers tell us about reality?

You attend a concert, and the performers play a piece that lifts your soul and sets it soaring. The music moves you so deeply that it literally makes the hair on your neck stand on end. You wonder how music can evoke such powerful emotions.

You visit a gallery and stand before a painting of such stunning color, depth, and substance that it takes your breath away and makes your heart beat faster.

You round the bend on a rugged mountain trail and stop dead in your tracks, awestruck by the vista before you. A glorious, snowcapped peak gleams in the sunlight, its grandeur reflected in a pristine lake rimmed with towering pines. You find yourself overcome with longings and aspirations you can neither identify nor explain.

You watch in rapt fascination as an Olympic skater glides, leaps, and spins with breathtaking grace and balance. As the performance ends, you and everyone in the stands spontaneously rise to cheer and applaud.

On some enchanted evening, you look across a crowded room and see a face that captivates you completely. You know at that moment you want to gaze upon that face the rest of your life.

In each of these settings you experience the mystery of beauty—immersion into the deep, inner pleasure we feel in response to certain combinations of form, color, texture, sound, or movement. For the purposes of our discussion in this chapter, beauty includes all objects, sights, sounds, or experiences that stir us to awe, elation, inspiration, enchantment, delight, or ecstasy. Beauty is what lifts life above the mundane and prosaic and gives it joy.

We are hard-pressed to explain why encounters with beauty affect us so profoundly. What is there about a song, a snow-clad peak, a work of art, or a face that so grips our hearts and thrills our souls? Despite the high place we give beauty in our lives, our attempts to define it fall short.

Explanations for Beauty

For the most part, we don't even try to define beauty; we merely explain it away as something altogether subjective. "Beauty is in the eye of the beholder," we say, meaning beauty has no objective reality but is merely a term we use to encompass people's differing aesthetic preferences. I find beauty in the mountains; you find it in the seashore. I enjoy classical music; you're into jazz. I appreciate the French Impressionists; you prefer Andy Warhol. I like colonial architecture; you are awed by the glass-and-steel lines of modern skyscrapers. Because we recognize such broadly differing preferences, most of us feel that standards for beauty are determined solely by personal taste.

Our variations in preference, however, are minor compared to the vast sea of agreement about what is beautiful and what is not. For example, almost everyone considers swans and butterflies beautiful but not bats and tarantulas. Most of us see beauty in an Alpine vista of soaring mountains but not in an ash-coated landscape devastated by a volcanic eruption. Opinions vary greatly over what constitutes beauty in the human body. Ideal physical characteristics for both sexes range all over the board. Yet there are certain people who so completely transcend our individualized ideals that they are universally recognized as beautiful. While the eyes of beholders may reveal differing individual preferences, these preferences are merely variations within great, common themes of beauty that virtually all people recognize.

Naturalists tend to explain beauty in terms of pragmatic function. What we call beauty in living creatures, they see as features that evolved only to protect and propagate the various species. To them the brilliant color of a flower has nothing to do with joy and delight; it is merely nature's signal to attract butterflies and bees to achieve cross-pollination.

Naturalists would deny that the feminine physical features of a woman we call beautiful were designed to produce aesthetic appreciation; rather, they attract men because they display her capacity to bear and nurture children. A man's broad shoulders, firm abs, and bulging biceps attract females simply because they display his ability to protect and provide. A peacock spreads its gorgeous plumage to attract a peahen. The splendid stripes of a tiger merely camouflage the animal as it stalks its prey in tall grass. To naturalists, what we call beauty is no mystery at all. It is the by-product of nature's practical means for propagating and preserving life on the planet.

Some philosophers have attempted to explain beauty in terms of harmony, symmetry, proportion, rhythm, and archetypes. To product designers, architects, and engineers, beauty is simply that which displays efficiency and functionality. Architect Frank Lloyd Wright's famous maxim "form follows function" summarized his belief that designing for efficiency tends to result in beauty. The supersonic Concorde aircraft that formerly flew from Paris to New York has been called the

> most beautiful machine ever built. . . . It looked so exquisite because its shape was primarily dictated not by a designer, but by the immutable laws of physics themselves, the flow of air over its wings at both subsonic and supersonic speeds, the need to fit within its own supersonic shockwave, to outrun its

own sound, the need to pierce the thin air at nearly the speed of a fired bullet.[1]

Success at achieving utility gave the plane beauty as a natural by-product.

It is tempting to think that efficiency and functionality may provide the keys to the mystery of beauty. Things that function efficiently do tend to be what we call beautiful, whereas things that are clumsy or ineffective do not. Health is beautiful, while sickness and decay are not. Life is beautiful, and death is a horror. Harmony is beautiful, and dissonance is repelling. Order is beautiful, whereas chaos and imbalance make us uneasy and tense. Beauty seems to grow out of efficiency. We don't tend to find it in waste, decay, brokenness, or malfunction.

This explanation holds much truth, but it admits too many exceptions to be the whole story. Efficient function often exists independent of beauty. Two people may be equally strong, healthy, hardworking, and efficient, but one may have beauty while the other does not. Despite architect Wright's theory, the popularity of Victorian and antebellum architecture tells us that many people find beauty in ornamentation that has no practical function at all. If efficiency and functionality are beautiful, why do most people find even harmless spiders hideous? Music has no apparent utilitarian function at all, yet the pleasure it brings is so lavish and spectacular that our response is often nothing short of ecstatic. If death is a horror, why is no season of the year more beautiful than autumn, which owes its spectacular color to dying tree leaves? If life itself is intrinsically beautiful, how do we explain our extreme revulsion to a colony of teeming maggots?

An airtight explanation for beauty eludes us. Why we get such enjoyment from seeing certain forms, hearing certain sounds, and feeling certain textures remains a baffling question. Our purpose here, however, is not to answer that question. It is to show that while we cannot understand or define beauty, it is not an illusion. It is not solely utilitarian, and it is not subjective. We are convinced that beauty exists as an objective reality, and nothing within nature will account for it.

Turning Reality Wrong Side Out

Naturalistic explanations for beauty do not work because they tend to turn reality wrong side out. Naturalism reduces everything in nature to a mechanical function, but reality presents itself to us the other way around. To demonstrate the point, the meaning of an analog clock is not in its gears and springs, but on its face where it displays the time. The gears and springs are the innards, the working mechanisms hidden behind the face that provide the movements necessary to give the face its meaning. But naturalists see the mechanics that keep nature running as the sum total of reality, whereas believers in theistic creation see the mechanics as only the means to achieve the purpose for which things exist.

The mechanics are merely the innards, while all the meaning is found in the function that the mechanics produce. The naturalists' philosophy is wrong side out because it mistakes the mechanics for the essence.

To illustrate, consider your computer. The electrical impulses, printed circuits, drives, disks, and chips inside your computer are what make it work, but they are not its essence. Its essence is found in its purpose, which gives it meaning. What gives your computer purpose and meaning is how it helps you work, learn, compute, and communicate. The mechanics are important not for their own sake but only because they give you what you see on your screen and print on your printer. The mechanics are the means of producing the computer's purpose. They are not the true essence of the computer.

The naturalists' universe is wrong side out because they insist that there is nothing more to it than the machinery that keeps it running. Its mechanics are its essence. The blind, purposeless functioning of all nature is to them the sum total of reality. Naturalists do not admit to meaning and purpose in the universe because such an admission implies that meaning and purpose came first, and the mechanics were designed to achieve them. This implication requires a designer, something the naturalistic worldview cannot allow. To maintain their philosophy of reality, naturalists must assert that the accidental, meaningless mechanisms that keep the universe running are all the reality that exists.

Naturalistic philosophy leaves no place for beauty. In

seeing the universe solely as a purposeless mechanism, naturalists lose all that gives it beauty; they can see no truth deeper than what they find in the analysis of its parts. They find no meaning or purpose behind the analysis, and the result is a loss of mystery and art. Doggedly consistent naturalists cannot admit the grandeur of a snowcapped mountain because grandeur is a concept that requires more meaning than mere mechanics can provide. All they can allow themselves to see in the mountain are solidified minerals of the earth's crust broken and thrust upward by random geologic forces. They cannot allow any sense of art or meaning to the arrangement of the forms, textures, light, and colors of the peak. They cannot let themselves feel any sense of awe or delight in the extravagant forms of nature. They must close their minds to any invitation to lay aside their analytic X-ray lens and join the dance.

To sit down to a breakfast of bacon, eggs, honey, and milk is a great pleasure for most of us. But if all we see on our table are fatty slivers from the stomach of a mud-wallowing mammal, the ovulation of a large fowl coagulated by heat, sticky secretions from the reproductive organs of plants mixed with the saliva of an insect, and the discharge from the mammary gland of a ruminating mammal, we are likely to lose our appetites. Yet this is the breakfast naturalists sit down to every morning. This outlook, which reduces to mechanics all that gives delight to the senses, reflects their philosophy of all nature. When they look out their window at what theists see as trees, shrubs, flowers, and grass, naturalists see masses of tentacles, follicles, and fibers clutching the earth, sucking nutrients from it like parasitic lampreys. When naturalists look at a spring leaf, they do not see the glory of existence in its form, color, and texture. Instead, they see only the chemicals and mechanics of sap, photons, veins, and tissues. The green of the leaf does not inspire them to wonder and delight; it is merely the mechanical result of photosynthesis turning light rays into chlorophyll and has no more claim to beauty than the putrid green excretion of an infected bile duct.

The Naturalistic Inconsistency

You may think it's pretty presumptuous of us to portray the way all naturalists look at nature. You are right; it is. What we describe above is the way naturalists *should* see nature if they remain consistent with their philosophy. But the fact is, despite holding to a philosophy that logically excludes beauty, most naturalists do respond to beauty much as theists do. They can hardly help it. Intellectually, they may explain the spectrum of color inherent in sunlight in strictly scientific terms as the product of a mechanistic universe, but they are as likely as theists to feel delight in a sunset or a rainbow.

Here is the reason: beauty is a reality so much stronger than naturalistic philosophy that it simply storms past their intellect and acts directly on their emotions. It's likely that most naturalists have not thought through their position to its logical conclusion. They don't realize that they cannot remain consistent naturalists and yet believe in beauty. But for those unfortunate enough to have a strong commitment to both consistency and naturalistic philosophy, the light of beauty can no longer shine.

If you think we are overstating the case, read the pitiable lament of scientist and poet George John Romanes, a believer in God and creation until he abandoned his faith to become a disciple of Darwin:

> I am not ashamed to confess that with this virtual negation of God the universe to me has lost its soul of loveliness . . . when at times I think, as think at times I must, of the appalling contrast between the hallowed glory of that creed which once was mine, and the lonely mystery of existence as I now find it,—at such times I shall ever feel it impossible to avoid the sharpest pang of which my nature is susceptible.[2]

Romanes expressed the tragic despair of those who allow their philosophy to distort their view of reality. When he turned to naturalism, he turned the universe wrong side out. The innards came to the surface, and all he could see was the viscera of reality—the mechanical workings, the chugging, pulsating engine of nature fueling itself on itself, producing nothing important, designed for no purpose, but running on aimlessly like a Rube Goldberg machine until it inevitably peters out. When Romanes excluded God from his world, all that could give meaning to its forms, textures, colors, and sounds evaporated. He was left in a lonely, darkened universe haunted by an illusion of beauty that his new philosophy forced him to reject.

Naturalists may regard beauty as an illusion, but it is an illusion that most of them cannot ignore. It is one of the few aspects of their mechanistic universe that may temporarily divert their minds from the tragic, ultimate oblivion of all things, including themselves. It's better to dance on the edge of the grave than to stare brooding into its darkness.

The direction that much art has taken in the past few generations tells us something about the despair of naturalism. There was a time when the goal of most artists was to display beauty. As Woody Allen has his character Gertrude Stein say in the film *Midnight in Paris*, "The artist's job is not to succumb to despair but to find an antidote for the emptiness of existence." When naturalistic philosophy became dominant, however, much art became increasingly pointless, chaotic, despairing, nihilistic, and consciously devoid of beauty. The philosophy of meaninglessness leeched the vibrance from the brushes of modern painters and the harmony from the scores of modern composers. In their despair, they dismissed beauty as an illusion that cannot hide the dark void they believe will ultimately engulf all things.

Here is the bottom-line reason that beauty cannot exist in a truly naturalistic world: beauty implies an ideal. The concept of beauty suggests standards that an object must meet to achieve perfection. The more nearly an object matches the ideal for its kind, the more beautiful it is. But in a naturalistic, accidental world with no absolutes, no such ideals or standards are possible. What is, merely is; there is no such thing as what ought to be. We must have a standard that defines what ought to be before we can evaluate whether a form meets that standard. In a world without God, all forms and functions are accidental and, according to evolution, in a state of perpetual change, drifting on the endless currents of natural selection, mutation, and adaptation. We cannot freeze the evolutionary frame at any moment in this chain of continual flux and claim that a given form is ideal.

The Theist's Explanation

How do theists explain the ecstatic human response to a Schubert symphony, a Raphael painting, or the luminescent glow of a West Texas sunset? What did the Christian poet Samuel Taylor Coleridge mean when he agreed with a fellow tourist that "majestic" was just the right adjective to describe a Scottish waterfall?[3] C. S. Lewis points out in *The Abolition of Man* that when naturalist thinkers analyze this kind of emotional response to any object in nature, they believe we are saying nothing meaningful about the object itself, but "actually we are only saying something about our own feelings."[4] Naturalists assert that such feelings in response to nature are merely subjective, that nothing about the waterfall itself is inherently majestic. They claim that when we express such feelings, we are merely describing the subjective state of our emotions rather than saying anything meaningful about the object that aroused the emotion.

Such feelings are absurd and inexplicable, however, unless the waterfall has some inherent quality that elicits the awe the viewer feels. What quality can a waterfall, a sunset, or a mountain possess that makes one's feelings of awe or majesty appropriate? Naturalists will say that these geologic and atmospheric features have no such inherent quality. They will turn them wrong side out, expose their innards, and say that the mountain's craggy surface thrusting upward toward the clouds is merely the result of tectonic mechanics—the natural geologic forces moving beneath the crust of the earth. The waterfall is nothing more than gravity's inevitable effect on flowing liquid at the point where a river channel ends at a precipice. If this concept of nature is accurate, how do naturalists explain the lofty feelings these natural geologic phenomena evoke? Such feelings make no sense in a totally naturalistic universe. Something more is involved here than geology and gravity.

The mountain may be a work of art. That is, a creator may have purposefully willed its form to evoke in us a specific effect. We may not know exactly what effect this creator intended, but we can extrapolate a possibility from feelings common to so many people that they may be considered universal. To most viewers, mountains evoke feelings of upward aspiration, of majesty, of a mystical reaching for something above ourselves. Perhaps you yourself have had a similar response when standing at the foot of a lofty peak. Perhaps the mountain was created to be a visual metaphor for our longing to touch some quality beyond our limited experience. Like Plato's shadows in a cave, mountains, sunsets, and beautiful music and art may be dim hints of greater realities that exist in a supernatural realm above our own. The beauties we experience in nature may be echoes from beyond nature telling us that something more exists than what we see in our world—and what we see in our world are projected images of that greater reality.

It is those dreamers among us, those incurable romantics, who come closest to the truth about the nature of our world. It is in those moments when we feel the grandeur of the mountain, when the landscape is breathtaking, when the tree leaves glow with magical light, when the music seems to tingle with the essence of life, when the face we gaze upon seems to glow with the ethereal light of a goddess that the veil is lifted and we see reality for what it is. The naturalists' analytic lens that dismisses such experiences as romantic illusions misses reality by a tree-lined, flower-strewn, brook-rippling, bird-chirping country mile.

Yes, we know all about the other side of nature—death, decay, pain, heartache, cancers, grief, heart attacks, hurricanes, floods, tornadoes, and earthquakes. These woes are terrible, but they are only temporary blights on reality, not reality itself. For several years my route to work took me (Tom) across a metal truss bridge spanning the Colorado River near Austin, Texas. Every inch of that bridge's surface is covered with rust. Even though I could not actually see the steel substance of the bridge because of its rust coating, I would never assert that the rust is the reality of the bridge. The truth about the bridge is the solid metal beneath the rust. The truth about creation is the glory beneath the blight that mars it. The romantics so ridiculed in our disenchanted secular world are really the ones with the clearest eyes. They see through the rust to the metal beneath. Their eyes penetrate the fog that clouds the vision of the rest of us. In seeing beauty for what it is, they see the truth about reality.

The Promise of Beauty

For all the longings beauty arouses in us, nothing in nature or art will fully answer. No melody, however sensitively performed or skillfully adorned with harmonies, satisfies the unnamed desires it stirs in our souls. No woman or man, however perfect in face and form, however delightful in personality, however lovely in spirit, however loving and devoted, quite fills the yearning of one heart to merge with another. Despite the longing we feel as we stand before a majestic peak, there is nothing about the mountain itself that we desire. The inherent quality of the mountain that arouses the longing is a shadow of something greater. The mountain is not the object we desire, but it does point us toward it.

These objects of beauty we find all around us are only shadows, though lovely ones, of a reality we desire, a reality that as yet is unseen, unheard, and unfelt. The beauty in nature stirs up a "memory" of something we were meant to enjoy but have never fully experienced. It's as if something hovers at the edge of our comprehension that requires a sense not yet developed in order to grasp it fully. Yet we can occasionally catch dim, fleeting glimpses of it through the five senses we do have.

Beauty calls with a siren's voice, and our longing to abandon all and chase after it is almost overwhelming. But we find that beauty is like the rainbow's end: it beckons but eludes. It's a shimmering soap bubble that vanishes in our grasp. In the presence of beauty, we are like a child with her nose pressed to the window of a toy store. We look and yearn, but a barrier prevents the full experience of what is before us. As much as we long to immerse ourselves in the beauty we see, we cannot do it. Even at the most intense moment of ecstasy in our experience of the symphony, the sunset, the painting, or the embrace, we realize that what we really long for is yet beyond. These wonderful things are only images of the real object of our desire, and that object remains as elusive as ever. Whatever it is we long for, beauty is not it. Beauty is merely a window opened to reveal it.[5]

In beauty we hear the chords of the supernatural reverberating within nature. Beauty invites us to see within nature and art that greater reality in which everything has its origin. Beauty in its fullness remains elusive because it emanates from a dimension that is closed off to us. We live within nature—a nature damaged by a primeval event known to theologians as the Fall (explained in the next chapter) that taints all the beauty that shines on it from the dimension of the supernatural. Yet beauty breaks through that distorting cloud and bathes all nature with a glory that declares the transcendent source of all things. The glimpses of beauty that invade our fallen world are tangible evidence that beauty in its fullness does exist. And that taste of beauty underscores the promise that we can ultimately ascend to that dimension and find the true object of our desire.

But not yet.

For now, our place is in our own world, where we have tasks to be done and duties to be performed before we can abandon all and pursue the beauty that so tantalizes us. Many poets, composers, and writers have eloquently expressed this overpowering yearning to abandon all and plunge headlong after beauty. *The Lord of the Rings* author J. R. R. Tolkien, in his short story "Leaf by Niggle," tells of a struggling artist so enamored with the beauty of leaves that he devotes his life to painting them. In time, however, the artist discovers that there is a greater beauty than the leaf and begins to paint the entire tree, then the forest, then the vista beyond the forest, then the light that gives glory to the vista. Niggle would devote every waking moment to the pursuit of his unfolding vision of beauty, but the recurring needs of his sickly neighbor frequently interrupt him and prevent him from ever finishing his painting. (Spoiler alert!) When Niggle arrives in the afterlife, he finds that the heavenly reality awaiting him is the country of his painting, now more glorious than his earthly ability could conceive or execute.

Sir Arthur Sullivan, the composer half of England's Gilbert and Sullivan team, in his stirring song "The Lost

Chord," portrays a weary composer sitting at an organ keyboard. As his fingers roam absently across the keys, he unwit-
tingly strikes an incredibly beautiful chord of music "like the
sound of a great Amen." The unearthly majesty of the chord
moves him to the core. As he puts it, the chord "came from
the soul of the organ, and enter'd into mine." He anxiously
tries to form the chord again, but to no avail. He finally realizes that it was not native to this earth, and though its echoes
will linger in his heart for the rest of his days, only in heaven
will he actually hear it again.[6]

In his poem "Stopping by Woods on a Snowy Evening,"
Robert Frost tells of passing a lovely, quiet woods during a
beautiful snowfall. The poet pauses as a compelling desire
urges him to enter the woods and immerse himself in its
idyllic serenity, to become one with it and find rest there.
But he cannot. He knows that the peace and loveliness that
draw him toward the woods are not yet his to claim. He and
the beauty he yearns for are of different worlds. His is the
world of duty to others like himself who must grapple with
adversity, pain, loss, grief, and want. He must maintain his
loyalty to fellow strugglers in the fallen world before he can
enter the perfect one. He sadly prods his horse forward, sigh-
ing as he passes:

The woods are lovely, dark and deep,
But I have promises to keep,
And miles to go before I sleep,
And miles to go before I sleep.[7]

The Image of Perfection

Christian theology provides the reason behind our desire for and alienation from beauty. It tells us that we are fallen creatures living in a fallen world. Originally, all nature emanated perfect, unsullied beauty, but it incurred damage, and the beauty became blighted. Now all beauty is, at best, flawed. No form is quite symmetrical, no face without blemish, no color pure, no balance perfect, no harmony without a touch of dissonance. A veil has been drawn between our world and the source of all perfect beauty.

A shadowy but tantalizing image of this perfect beauty that exists beyond the veil remains locked away in every human heart. This is why those dim rays of beauty that filter into our flawed world so arrest our attention and touch our emotions. At such moments we sense the existence of that original perfection that is now beyond our capacity to experience fully. A vision of what was meant to be flashes across the screen of our consciousness like a subliminal image, and we are hooked. We long for the full experience of what we can now only glimpse.

We can only glimpse it because the experience of beauty in its unfallen fullness is currently beyond the capacity of our fallen senses—but the flawed beauty that lingers in our world assures us of the greater reality that exists beyond the horizon. This awareness that beauty is real but currently unattainable is the source of our longing, our alienation, and our hope.

All beauty is an invitation to look beyond nature and art to embrace the greater reality that is the invisible object of our desire. The beauty of a magnificent painting calls us to engage the artist. The spine-tingling harmonies of a grand anthem point us toward the composer. A mountain sunrise, a delicate flower, the power and skill of an Olympic athlete, the grace of a soaring eagle—all draw us toward their designer.

Beauty not only points us toward God, it also reveals something of God's nature that even those who believe in him often find surprising. Just as reason shows the consistency of God and morality shows the character of God, beauty shows, if we can open our minds to see it, the emotion of God. Beauty is the joy, the delight, the smile, and the laughter of God—the ecstasy of God. Beauty reveals that God created us to experience more than just bare, mundane existence; he wants us to revel in supreme delight. Beauty shows that the world is infused with more meaning than mere mechanics can account for—meaning to be experienced in joy and ecstasy. We have hints and echoes and vibrations of it throughout all creation. These daily promises of ultimate beauty make life precious and worthwhile, even while we cope with the pains and disasters of this fallen world.

This truth about beauty highlights the tragedy of the naturalists. Their world of mechanistic and aimless function is a poor substitute for the hints of sublime reality that beauty promises. Naturalism is inadequate to account for beauty. Beauty growing out of naturalism is like a rose growing out of an ash heap. If the ash heap is all that exists, we have no way to account for the rose. Of course, the rose is easy to explain if we assume the ash heap is not all that exists—that beneath the ashes is fertile soil into which a seed was dropped from a source above it. And this is exactly the position of theists.

If you consider yourself an agnostic or an atheist, or even if you are a Christian who has doubts about your faith, we urge you to take a hard look at the possibility that beauty is no illusion. Beauty offers a strong hint that just outside our field of vision hovers a living power who cares for us and wants us to experience delight. God gave us beauty to lead us to him. It is in relationship to him that we experience the essence of all beauty.

QUESTIONS FOR THOUGHT AND DISCUSSION

1. Does beauty exist only in the eye of the beholder? Why or why not?

2. How do naturalists define beauty?

3. How does the naturalistic view of beauty turn reality "wrong side out"?

4. Why do naturalists resist the idea that beauty suggests meaning and purpose?

5. How do theists define beauty?

6. In what ways does beauty point to the supernatural? Have you ever had a fleeting sense that there was something more and something unobtainable behind your experience of beauty?

7. Why is beauty unable to satisfy the longings it arouses? What will satisfy those longings?

11

THE PATH TO KNOWING GOD

*How you can experience meaning
and fulfillment in your life*

Every human being comes into the world with three questions etched into his or her subconscious: *Who am I? Why am I here? Where am I going?* We feel restless and adrift until we discover the answers, which reveal to us our identity, our purpose, and our destiny. As we have demonstrated in this book, those who have taken the leap of faith into naturalism will find the answers to these three questions utterly unsatisfactory. Their responses must run something like this:

Who am I? I am the product of random forces operating mindlessly on self-existent, meaningless matter. Ultimately, I have no identity because I am merely a random assemblage of atoms with no more permanence or value than any other assemblage, whether it be a tree, a rock, a bug, a fungus, or anything else that exists.

Why am I here? Since the universe is the result of a mindless cosmic accident, it has no ultimate purpose. Since I also am a result of that mindless event, I have no ultimate purpose.

Where am I going? Destiny implies purposeful direction, and since purpose is an illusion in a mindless, accidental universe, I have no ultimate destiny. Like the universe itself, I am doomed to ultimate and permanent oblivion.

These answers are far from satisfying. It's no wonder that people steeped in naturalism keep searching for better alternatives in any new philosophy or psychological mindset that offers more attractive promises.

The Search for Transcendence

The longing for meaning and transcendence compels searchers to try many paths that lead to dead ends. For example, you may have been told that the answer lies inward instead of upward. You feel isolation and emptiness, the theory goes, not because you lack a transcendent God but because you have not found your true self. This search for self pervades our literature, our psychology, our movies, and even our humor. A scrawled sign taped to the door of an empty office read: "I've gone to find myself. If I should show up before I get back, just tell me to sit down and wait for me to return."

Popular psychology tells us that our upbringing, societal expectations, religious beliefs, and personal neuroses conspire to hide the true self beneath layers of distorting masks that we wear to make ourselves acceptable to those about us. These masks confuse us to the point that we don't know what is real about ourselves. We are told that when we strip away the masks and find the authentic self beneath them, our sense of alienation will disappear.

It doesn't work.

Self-assessment and self-realization do not fill the emptiness. While such exercises may have value as starting points for understanding our needs, simply finding our true self is not a solution. We are finite; the self has limits. Our hunger for meaning is greater than our ability to satisfy it. Even if we "find ourselves" and settle down to enjoy the discovery, the sense of satisfaction will not last. Sooner or later we will plumb the depths of self and discover that it is too shallow to provide lasting enjoyment or ultimate meaning.

You have probably already encountered the widespread approach to fulfillment that tells us to look neither upward nor inward but outward. It is encapsulated in a slogan from an old beer commercial that urges us to find fulfillment in materialism and hedonism: "You only go around once in life. So grab for all the gusto you can."[1] Fill the void in your life with toys, entertainment, prestige, pleasure, and achievements.

It doesn't work.

Stuff from the outside cannot satisfy the hunger on the inside. After we've tried it all, it all becomes insipid, repetitious, and meaningless, and we find ourselves singing that dreary refrain along with Peggy Lee: "Is that all there is? If that's all there is my friends, then let's keep dancing."[2]

It's the answer of despair, the conclusion that the emptiness is permanent and terminal. Nothing will fill it, so to smother our awareness of it we must "keep dancing." Focus on distractions. Move fast. Stay busy. Party hearty. Do anything, buy anything, try anything to keep from looking into that dark abyss in the soul.

It doesn't work.

Just as pains and growls force you to attend to an empty stomach, the pain of emptiness in the soul will eventually get your attention despite your most determined attempts to ignore it.

The Missing Piece

If we could create our own truth and validate it merely by believing it, we should be able to fill that void in the soul with whatever we truly believe will fill it. But it swallows everything we throw into it yet remains as empty as ever. We cannot create our own personal reality because a true reality already exists, and the void in the human heart derives its shape from this true reality. Like the missing piece of a jigsaw puzzle, no substitute will fit. Unless we find the one piece designed to fill the space, the picture remains incomplete.

Seventeenth-century philosopher Blaise Pascal identified this emptiness in the human heart, and we've come to refer to it as a "God-shaped vacuum."[3] Pascal realized that humankind's inner hunger can never be satisfied until it recognizes God as the missing piece meant to fill the emptiness. God is the ultimate absolute who brings meaning directly into the life of every man and woman. God in the human life is the keystone to the arch, the one stone that fits at the apex, bringing solidity to the entire structure and holding all other stones firmly in place.

We have demonstrated in this book how reason should lead us to recognize the inevitability of God's existence. We have explained that a confident step of rationally supported faith puts our trust in the certainty of that truth, bringing us face to face with the God who is the ultimate absolute and true origin of matter, life, beauty, and meaning. Now we want to remind you of what that God is like—or, if you do not already know this God, we'd like to introduce you to him. We want to explain the essence of his character and reveal what he desires from us and plans for us. By being in the right relationship with him, we find answers to the questions about our identity, purpose, and destiny. In knowing God intimately, we experience personally the truth that we can discover intellectually.

The Nature and Character of God

The Bible shows God to be completely different from the images of gods that dominate human history. His character can be described as absolute good and absolute love. He is not confined by a physical body, and his complete presence fills every nook and cranny in the universe. He is not the universe, however, nor is he one with the universe. He is separate from his creation just as an architect is separate from his building. He is all-powerful and all-knowing. He is by nature both personal and relational. Indeed, his very mode of being is relational. One of the great mysteries about God is that he exists as a Trinity—a living unity of three distinct personalities eternally bonded by love in an intimate relationship. This bond forms a oneness so close and intertwined that the three members of the Godhead are identified in the singular simply as God.

Just as married couples desire children, the three persons of the Godhead desired to expand and share the love that flows within their relationship. Acting on that desire, God created man and woman—creatures bearing his own likeness, creatures he could love and who could love him in return. He breathed his own Spirit into this first couple, placing his own life at the center of their being and filling their lives with meaning and love. He gave them the task of running and caring for the earth, which filled their lives with purpose. They accomplished this purpose by bearing within themselves the life of God, which gave them the will and power to fulfill their destiny. This intimate relationship with God not only completed this primeval couple, it also gave them immense joy. Their lives were full and complete because they were fulfilling the role for which they were designed. As a result, their lives overflowed with continual ecstasy and lavish delight.

This intimate, bonded relationship with each human has been God's intent from the time of creation. If you wonder how a being, even though he is God, could maintain a meaningful relationship with billions of people at the same time, well, so do we. Yet we do not find this phenomenon unbelievable because we humans create electronic devices that keep up with millions of transactions simultaneously. If megacompanies such as Google, Amazon, and global banks employ machines that perform such amazing multitasking, it is not incredible to think the supernatural God who created the universe and everything in it could do it infinitely better and faster.

The metaphors the Bible uses to picture the relationship between God and his people give us an idea of just how warm and close he intended that relationship to be. In some passages he portrays himself as a loving father, in others as a brother or a lover. Many passages portray God's relationship to his people as a marriage. The core idea within these various pictures is clear: God desires a relationship with us that is filled with all the joy and warmth of our closest human connections.

God intended love to be the dominating characteristic and driving force of all creation. He created men and women to be relational creatures who desire to expand and share the love he lavishes on them. We are designed to live not only in an upward relationship with God, but also in outward relationships with others. These connections can be as diverse as the neighbor who borrows a cup of sugar, the friendly competitiveness of a foursome on the golf course, the best friend who lends a sympathetic ear, the deep and delightful bond with children, or the intense commitment and ecstatic intimacy of marriage. We thrive on such relationships because we were created for connection with each other.

This intertwining dance of love with God and others is what gives meaning to human life. As long as the first created couple maintained their relationship with God, his love flowed through them and enabled them to remain in perfect relational harmony with each other and the rest of creation. Bearing the life of God within themselves, their lives had ultimate meaning, and they were fulfilled. There was no missing piece.

The Broken Relationship

Obviously, something has gone wrong. The idyllic picture we have painted of God's love bathing all the world in blissful harmony and relational fulfillment is far from the reality we experience today. If God intended us to have perfect relationships, why do they so often go wrong? Why are joy and fulfillment so elusive? Why is it such a struggle to find God? The answer is that God's original intent has been thwarted in a tragic event that Christians know as the Fall. If you have any acquaintance with biblical theology, you probably have at least a vague familiarity with this story. In case you don't, we will explain it briefly.

The Fall was a mortal, self-inflicted wound that occurred when the first created man and woman misused their God-given freedom. As most people know, no one can be forced to love. In a love relationship, both parties must freely choose to love before love can be authentic. Although God made humans for the very purpose of loving him and bearing his essence, he did not force himself on them. The relationship was purely voluntary. The man and woman were free to choose God and all the joy, love, fulfillment, and ecstasy he brought to them, or they could choose self and go their own way without him. Giving humans this freedom was a bold and precarious move on God's part, but it was the only way love could be real and meaningful.

Tragedy invaded the earth's idyllic environment when the couple listened to the voice of an adversary of God known at Satan. Satan is a created being of immense power. Prior to the creation of the first humans, he had exercised his God-given freedom and rebelled against God. As a result, he was banished permanently from God's presence. Motivated either by vindictiveness or a desire to rule the earth himself, Satan deceived the first human couple into rejecting God and going out on their own. In the name of freedom, God honored their choice. He withdrew himself from their lives and left them to find their own way. When God withdrew, not only did their lives go out of kilter, nature itself went out of kilter. Storms, floods, earthquakes, pain, disease, alienation, sorrow, and death entered the scene and ruined their perfect world.

Suddenly, the lives of the human couple were empty. Without God, they were alienated from their purpose and lost their significance. They and their children after them became focused primarily on self, and it took only a few generations for almost all awareness of God's existence to disappear. Humans had no idea what they had lost or where to look for it—no concept of who they were or what they were meant for. Estranged from God, they were left with that ravenous void in their souls and a compulsion to fill it with anything that might alleviate their craving for meaning, purpose, and fulfillment.

Without the stability of that primary, vital relationship with God, all human relationships went askew. Men and women became like spokes in a damaged bicycle wheel, tenuously connected at the rim but loose and flailing aimlessly because they were disconnected from the hub. No longer could they function in a secure and reliable way. They still had relationships with the other spokes on the rim, but those connections were also uncertain because they had lost their stabilizing connection to a central entity that gave all relationships purpose. Lacking attachment to God, people lost their point of reference for good relationships with each other. People became their own gods, looking to themselves as their own absolute and fiercely protecting their own self-interests.

Naturally, these separate points of reference did not mesh well with each other. As people staked out their own territory and tenaciously protected it, they pushed themselves apart from each other. Each focused primarily on his or her own wants and needs, which fostered the pride, selfishness, alienation, anger, and hatred that have infected the human family throughout history.

Restoring the Relationship

When the first couple turned away from God, you might expect that he would have washed his hands of them and directed his affection toward a more grateful civilization somewhere on the far side of the galaxy. Amazingly, he did the opposite. Like the mythical Greek sculptor Pygmalion, God had fallen in love with his created humans and could not bear to lose them. He knew that by rejecting him, the source of life, they had consigned themselves to death. Therefore, he set out to perform a daring rescue.

The second member of the Godhead, whom the world knows as Jesus Christ, came to earth, and took the form of a man, the God-man. As an unfallen human with no sins of his own, Christ took on himself the guilt of humanity's sins and died a horrific death on a Roman cross, thus paying the penalty for all sins. By this act humanity was freed from the guilt of sin, which enables each of us to choose eternal life by explicitly accepting Christ's sacrifice for our own sins. This astounding act has much more meaning than we can explain here, but in summary, let it suffice to say that Christ's sacrifice disarmed death and restored to doomed humankind the right to reestablish a relationship with God.

Many who are seeking truth in the Bible find their path

blocked by questions about the severity of God. Why would he require such a brutal sacrifice before he could forgive us? That is a fair question, and it has an answer. But to address it here would take us beyond the available space and scope of this book. If that question troubles you, we urge you to consult the pastors or teachers in a Bible-centered church for answers. Whatever questions you may have about the severity of God, please don't fail to consider this one: What could possibly cause a perfect God to endure the terrible ordeal of crucifixion other than a deep, unfathomable love? The Crucifixion shows that God loved us so much he was willing to enter with us into the mess we made of our world. He willingly suffered the same kind of death we inflicted on ourselves.

The emergence of the living Christ from his tomb, known as the Resurrection,* was the guarantee that any person who chose to come back to God would be restored to a life of renewed relationship with him.

So why isn't it working? you may ask. If God came to earth to restore his loving relationship with us, why isn't it restored? Why is he still so hard to find? Why do people still stumble around the planet ignorant of God, searching for whatever they can find to fill the void in their souls?

The first answer is found in our freedom and God's respect for it. He does not invade our space. Through the rebellion of the first couple in Eden, we humans chose to

---

* Although the claim that Christ was resurrected from death prevents many from believing in the God of Christianity, there exists ample evidence of its truth. For a complete listing and thorough exploration of this evidence, see Josh McDowell and Sean McDowell, *Evidence That Demands a Verdict* (Nashville, TN: Thomas Nelson, 2017).

push God out of our lives. He will not violate that choice by pushing himself back in. He has left abundant evidence of his existence in nature and dropped telling clues of it from the supernatural realm (as we noted in the previous chapter). But he remains behind the veil, knowing that if he forces his presence on us, we will have no choice but to believe, and the freedom he has given us to choose him will be compromised. We must repudiate our choice to follow self and express our desire for a restored relationship with God before he will move back into our lives.

A second reason God is hard to find is because the evils that invaded our world at the Fall have fogged the intellectual atmosphere, dulling our ability to apprehend truth. Evil distracts, distorts, and disguises reality, obscuring our vision of what is right and good. Seeing real truth through the fog requires diligent searching and a commitment to act on truth when we find it.

A third factor that makes God seem distant and hidden is our own self-centeredness. As a result of the Fall, our own ambitions, felt needs, and pride in achievement became so much the focus of our lives that we resist the intrusion of a higher power that might impose restraints on our self-serving desires.

The Problem of Evil

Humanity's choice of self over God also answers the question that almost every atheist or agnostic asks: *If God is both good and all-powerful, why is there so much evil in the world?* They reason that either he is not good or he would eradicate evil, or he is not all-powerful and cannot eradicate it. Either way, they find him not worth their belief.

For the true answer to this persistent question, we return to the fact that God gave us free will. The first humans used their free will to ignore God's warning and disobey him. Their disobedience signaled their rejection of God. Remaining true to his promise of freedom, he withdrew from their lives. The loss of his benevolent, protective power opened the gates to Satan and his malignant influences, which rushed in and wreaked havoc on nature. Despite this invasion, God had to honor the freedom he had given humanity, which meant he had to let their choice stand. To correct it would have meant their freedom was a sham. Consider how you would respond if God stepped in and prevented or corrected every mistake you made. You would soon feel like a puppet on strings or a controlled drone with no meaningful will of your own. Evil is here because our human choices have meaning. We exercised our free choice by opening the door to evil, which means evil is here because of us, not because of God.

Despite the fact that humankind messed up God's perfect world, he keeps turning the wheels and shifting the gears to work in our favor. Just as we chose to bring evil into a world of good, God now offers us the option to bring good back into a world of evil. God can make this offer despite humanity's sin because he took the brunt of the world's evil upon himself when he came into this fallen world and allowed himself to be tortured and murdered by the forces of evil. As a result of his death and Resurrection, he offers us the right to invite him back into our lives and restore the lost relationship, thus finding authentic love and meaning despite the ravages of a world infested with evil and death.

Given the Fall and its consequences, we can see why God is now harder to find. But we can also see that it is not God's doing. As the bumper sticker reads, "If you feel far from God, guess who moved." Despite the abundance of evidences of God's existence, we fallen humans are too caught up in ourselves, too distracted by our desires, too numbed by our secular preoccupations to see him clearly. Just as animals do not understand the meaning of a pointing finger, we don't understand the many clues in nature that point to God's existence. But that relentless love of his does not leave us solely to our own feeble devices. Even as we search for God, he pursues us, silently nudging events and manipulating circumstances to prod us toward him. Though we often remain blind to him, he is at all times as near as our next breath, ready at our invitation to enter our lives and fill the emptiness in our hearts.

Reason helps us to find God intellectually and gives us a rational foundation for faith, but reason is not where we actually experience God. As Pascal said, "It is the heart which experiences God, and not the reason."[4] The rational mind affirms God's existence and then passes the torch to the heart. The heart is where we experience life's fullness and enjoy all the beauty, joy, and love that gives it meaning. The human heart can find peace only when the God who loves us dearly returns to it and fills it with his love.

The Certainty of God's Love

It is not surprising that minds steeped in rationalism want to reject the reality of God's existence. The account of a supernatural creator of the universe who took on a human body and was executed and raised from the dead does not fit the thinking modes of twenty-first-century sophisticates. They see it as just another of many ancient myths telling of dying gods and human sacrifices to woo or appease alienated deities.

This resemblance of the Christ story to ancient myths is actually a strong indication of its truth. The theme of sacrifices and dying gods persists in mythology because it addresses something that has always been apparent to fallen humanity. People have always sensed the gravity of their alienation to whatever gods they worshiped and dimly realized that only the sacrifice of a god or an extraordinary human could bring about reconciliation. All such myths were prefiguring shadows that recognized the human dilemma and anticipated the solution.

At a specific point, however, a historical event occurred that fulfilled in reality the pattern of the myths. God actually did come down from heaven to live on earth as a man and be executed for the wrongs of the human race. In three days he came to life again and ascended to heaven, disabling the power of death and ripping away the veil that separated us from God.

Why should we accept the Christian story alone as true while rejecting the similar myths that precede it? Because it differs from the others as a shout differs from its echo or a tree from its shadow. This tree is firmly rooted in history. The events of the Christian story occurred at a specific time and place and were corroborated as accurate by historians with no stake in the story's veracity—even by historians hostile to Christianity. Furthermore, the coming of Christ and many of the events in his life were predicted in writing—even down to such details as the time and place—centuries before they occurred.[5]

The claim that a supernatural God invaded nature, died, and rose again is astounding and seriously out of sync with the spirit of our secular age, but we have more reasons for believing it than not. We must not make the mistake of waiting for all the details to be explained before we allow belief to kick in. And we who already believe must not let unexplained minor details cause us to reconsider convictions that are buttressed by towering monolithic truths. When probing such enormous realities, we are like the blind men feeling the elephant. Our perspective is too limited to encompass the whole truth. We will always wrestle with troubling questions about God, such as the existence of pain, the concept of hell, or seeming (but minor) contradictions in the Bible.

These questions have excellent and helpful answers available to the person willing to seek them. But even when the explanations don't fill all the gaps in our comprehension, we must remember that we cannot expect to understand God any more than Loren Eiseley's orb spider could understand him. Often our objections to God are based on the assumption that he should think as we do—that he should have set up the world just as we think it ought to be. When we encounter a world that differs from our own ideal, doesn't it seem a bit presumptuous to banish its creator to nonexistence? Surely it's at least remotely possible that the world may exist as it is because its creator is a God whose mind is superior to our own. The only rational stance is to allow perplexing peripheral questions to be absorbed by our rational faith in the larger truth: God is a logical necessity; he defines reality; he died for you; he loves you dearly and unconditionally.

As we wonder why God does not reveal himself and his will more clearly, we must remember that originally he did. Before the Fall, God gave humans full access to his mind, and there were no ambiguities about right and wrong, no unanswered questions about his will, and no gaps in our relationship with him. We must remind ourselves that it was we humans who shut the door against God, and he has honored our choice by not invading our lives but leaving us with the autonomy we demanded. Then at great cost to himself, he offered a way out of the mess that resulted.

Throughout most of history, people have had little problem believing in a supernatural realm inhabited by God or gods. Widespread rejection of anything supernatural came on the scene with the rationalists' overconfidence in empiricism, which demanded "show me" proof before belief was allowed. When scientists grew bold enough to declare that what they could observe and test was all that could exist, the supernatural was demoted to the level of superstition. The modern age looked back on previous ages with the kind of condescension the enlightened tend to inflict on the ignorant. The attitude was that those poor people back then did not know any better, but we now stand in a position to pass judgment on the beliefs dominant in past ages. This attitude is not unique to our age. Every age tends to think its own viewpoint is superior to those of the past. Even the postmodernists have great confidence in their viewpoint that dismisses all viewpoints as hopelessly skewed.

We agree that viewpoints can skew objectivity and admit that we all have them. It seems clear, however, that the universe presents to us truths so monolithic that they tower above all viewpoints. Perhaps we cannot pull our feet completely out of the mire of modernism's overconfidence in empiricism or postmodernism's distrust of all truth claims, but we can see truths looming above us much larger than reason can comprehend. The fog of the secularisms surrounding us may blur our sight, but no fog can completely obscure the firm outline of the ultimate absolute. It is there in plain sight to be seen if only we will allow ourselves to see it.

There you have it. The ultimate absolute is also your personal absolute. Incredible as it may seem, the God of the universe loves you personally, and he wants to win you to himself. He wants to fulfill you completely and bring into your life meaning and joy beyond imagining. He is not only the absolute for the universe; he is also the absolute for your life and happiness. He is waiting for you to embrace him fully or invite him in.

Josh's Personal Story: "How I Came to Believe"

Believe me, I (Josh) understand how all this may sound to you. I identify with any impulse you may feel to doubt what we have presented in this book or even to reject it out of hand. Been there, done that. I spent much of my early life searching in all the wrong places for my identity, purpose, and destiny.

First, I threw myself into religion, going to church morning, afternoon, and evening, but something was still missing. Soon I gave up on religion as an empty and meaningless superstition. I looked for answers in education, but I quickly found that the university professors had just as many unanswered questions as I did. Then I tried prestige, but the glory of being elected to student offices and becoming a big man on campus soon faded, and I was still empty inside.

While in college, I came into contact with a group of about eight students and a couple of faculty members who seemed to have it all together. They had an easy confidence and firm convictions but not a trace of arrogance. They obviously cared for each other and even for others outside their group. I was drawn to these people and soon made friends with them.

As I sat talking with some of them, I faced a young woman and asked her straight out, "Tell me why you are so different from the others on this campus. What changed your lives?"

She looked me in the eye and uttered a name that one rarely hears on a university campus except in derision or as an expletive: "Jesus Christ."

I'm afraid my response was less than courteous. Jesus Christ, God, religion—I had grown past all that. Maybe gullible, superstitious, uneducated people easily swayed by their compelling needs could believe such hokum, but not me. Not anymore. I would not believe what my intellect rejected, and I told the young woman as much.

To my surprise, my new friends threw down the gauntlet. They challenged me to examine the evidence—to explore objectively the claim that Jesus Christ is the Son of God and that the Bible is God's Word and is trustworthy. At first I thought it was a joke, but when I saw that they were serious, I took them up on their challenge. After all, I was a prelaw student. I knew something about evidence, and I would soon show them that their whole religion was based on a hoax.

You can guess the rest of the story. I looked everywhere for evidence to show that the Bible cannot be trusted. The task proved much harder than I had anticipated, and the search began to consume me. After months of exhaustive research in the US, Europe, and the Middle East, I had to admit that the Old and New Testament documents were the most reliable writings in all antiquity. At the end of my search, I found myself standing face to face with the claims of Christ.

As you can see, it was not the Bible or historical evidence of its accuracy that initially drew me to God. It was his love shining through the lives of a handful of Christians who accepted me and cared about me. God's love reached out to draw me into a relationship with my Christian friends and through them to Christ himself. The hard, objective evidence convinced my mind that the Jesus who lived two thousand years ago was indeed the one, true God. Yet it wasn't the evidence—it was his love that tugged at my heart and drew me toward him. Examining the evidence merely removed the obstacles to belief and convinced me I had to make a decision.

The result of my search left me with a pivotal question. Since I was convinced that Christ is who he claimed to be, how was I going to respond? He was knocking at the door of my life and saying, "I love you. Let me come in, and you will discover the very meaning of life itself and find the purpose and destiny you have long searched for." That's exactly what I did.

I discovered that truth is not an abstract idea or a philosophical concept. Truth is a person. Truth resides innately within the character of God, and we experience truth in relationship with God incarnate, Jesus Christ. God himself is the answer to our search for meaning, identity, purpose, fulfillment, destiny, and love. He is the ultimate answer to all our questions, the object of all our longings. That's as true for you as it is for me.

If you are already a believer, I hope what we have shared in this book has been an encouragement to you and has helped to assuage any doubts you have had. If you have come to this book from a naturalist perspective, I hope what we have shared has helped to remove obstacles to belief and shown you that there can be only one answer to your search for truth. That answer is the one true God who is objectively real and is the ultimate absolute of the universe.

If you have come to believe in God but don't know where to go from here, we urge you to seek a church that still holds firmly to the foundational truths of the Bible. A minister will show you the way to learn more about the truths of Christianity and the way to enter the living organism we know as the church.

As you continue on your quest, you may find it helpful to pray the prayer I prayed if it truly reflects the desire of your heart as it did mine: "My God in heaven, I need you. Open my heart to the truth you would have me find. Thank you for dying on the Cross for me. I want to trust you as my Savior and invite you into my life. Make me the type of person you created me to be. In Christ's name, amen."

QUESTIONS FOR THOUGHT AND DISCUSSION

1. What are the three big questions that seem to be etched on every human heart?

2. What are some of the wrong places people often look for answers to these questions? Why don't these answers work?

3. What is the missing piece in the human heart?

4. What does it mean to say that God is a relational being?

5. What prompted the Fall? How did the Fall affect our relationships with God and others?

6. Why is God so hard to find even after he provided for a restored relationship with him? Which of the obstacles mentioned in this chapter have interfered with your own relationship with God?

7. How do we know the Christ story is not just another myth?

ACKNOWLEDGMENTS

Few books would ever become airborne without the wind beneath their wings provided by the talents of numerous specialists. This book is no exception. We willingly express our gratitude to several whose contributions have helped to shape or enhance these pages.

First, we thank former Josh McDowell Ministry CEO Don Kencke and his wife, Judy, for seeing the need to update and expand our 2003 book *In Search of Certainty* and suggesting direction and resources for the rewrite. Little did they know their efforts would result in what is essentially an all-new book.

We thank the present management team of JMM, including CEO Duane Zook and US Publications and Resource Director Dave Bottorff for seeing the value of the book, guiding the collaborative process between the authors, and managing the publication, business details, and creative growth of the project.

We are grateful to the Tyndale team of Jon Farrar and

Jonathan Schindler for their management of the publishing process. We thank Tyndale's editor Donna Berg for her editorial partnership and thorough work on the manuscript to ensure that what we wrote was always what we meant to say. We also thank copyeditors Deborah King and Kathleen Belcher and proofreaders Cheryl Warner and Claire Lloyd for their eagle eyes in scouring the manuscript for errant punctuation and grammatical infractions. We thank Jennifer Phelps for the cover and interior design. We are also grateful to the many Tyndale House specialists for handling the uncountable but vital details required to bring a book to the market—layout, production, marketing, and promotion.

We express our gratitude to a mix of ministers and laypersons who read all or specialized parts of the manuscript at various stages and offered valuable feedback. These readers include Gene Shelburne, Ashton Lewis, Greg Hargis, Lyndon Latham, Sherrinda Ketchersid, Tye Polk, Larry Branum, and MaryBeth Berry. We thank each of you for graciously allowing us to inflict the early drafts on you.

In the shaping of chapter 1, we gratefully acknowledge the influence of Canadian philosopher Charles Taylor's milestone book *A Secular Age*, as digested by James K. A. Smith in his excellent *How (Not) to Be Secular*.

To each of you we express our deep appreciation for your help in bringing this book about.

NOTES

Chapter 1: An Odd Thing Happened When We Got Rid of God

1. Nicola Benn, comment on Rainn Wilson, "Why Is Talking about God So Awkward?" Beliefnet, accessed January 30, 2017, http://www.beliefnet .com/entertainment/rainn-wilson/why-is-talking-about-god-awkward.aspx #wxCtTDoa0xHjkoZm.99.
2. Tressa Mizer, comment on Wilson, "Why Is Talking about God So Awkward?"
3. Richard Dawkins, *The Selfish Gene*, 40th anniversary edition (Oxford: Oxford University Press, 2016), 433.
4. Charles Taylor, *The Secular Age*, quoted by James K. A. Smith in *How (Not) to Be Secular: Reading Charles Taylor* (Grand Rapids: Eerdmans, 2014), 27. We acknowledge our debt in the shaping of this chapter to the monumental work of Charles Taylor with his analysis of secularism and its effect on today's culture, as filtered through James K. A. Smith's digest of it in *How (Not) to Be Secular*.
5. Richard Dawkins, *The Blind Watchmaker: Why the Evidence of Evolution Reveals a Universe without Design* (New York: W. W. Norton, 1996), 6.
6. Carl Sagan, *Cosmos: A Personal Voyage*, episode 1, "The Shores of the Cosmic Ocean," 1980, video, 3:15, https://ihavenotv.com/the-shores -of-the-cosmic-ocean-cosmos-a-personal-voyage.
7. George Bernard Shaw, "George Bernard Shaw Quotes," BrainyQuote, accessed August 25, 2020, https://www.brainyquote.com/quotes/george _bernard_shaw_155945.
8. "Depression Is on the Rise in the US, Especially among Young Teens," ScienceDaily, October 30, 2017, https://www.sciencedaily.com/releases /2017/10/171030134631.htm.

9. "Increase in Suicide Mortality in the United States, 1999–2018," Centers for Disease Control and Prevention, April 2020, https://www.cdc.gov /nchs/products/databriefs/db362.htm.

10. "Suicide and Self-Harm Injury," Centers for Disease Control and Prevention, last reviewed January 6, 2022, https://www.cdc.gov/nchs/fastats/suicide .htm.

11. Julian Baggini, "Yes, Life without God Can Be Bleak. Atheism Is about Facing Up to That," *The Guardian*, March 9, 2012, https://www.theguardian .com/commentisfree/2012/mar/09/life-without-god-bleak-atheism.

12. Mike Stoller and Jerry Leiber, "Is That All There Is?" lyrics posted at Genius, accessed August 27, 2020, https://genius.com/Peggy-lee-is-that -all-there-is-lyrics.

13. James K. A. Smith, *How (Not) to Be Secular: Reading Charles Taylor* (Grand Rapids, MI: Eerdmans, 2014), 14.

14. Julian Barnes, quoted in Smith, *How (Not) to Be Secular*, 66.

15. Anxious Anne, in Richard Wade, "Ask Richard: Atheist Haunted by the Fear of Death," Friendly Atheist, August 23, 2010, https://friendlyatheist .patheos.com/2010/08/23/ask-richard-atheist-haunted-by-the-fear -of-death/.

16. Peter Steele, quoted in Mick O'Shea, *Cemetery Gates: Saints and Survivors of the Heavy Metal Scene* (Plexus Publishing, 2013).

Chapter 2: The Need for Rock-Solid Standards

1. Cadie Thompson, "United Airlines Apologizes after Sending Woman to San Francisco instead of Paris," Business Insider, May 8, 2017, http://www .businessinsider.com/united-sends-woman-to-san-francisco-instead-of-paris -2017-5.

2. Claudia Koonz, *The Nazi Conscience* (Cambridge, MA: Harvard University Press, 2005).

3. G. K. Chesterton, *Orthodoxy* (Garden City, NY: Image Books, 1959), 29.

4. C. S. Lewis, *The Abolition of Man* (New York: HarperCollins, 2001), 81.

Chapter 3: The Troublesome Wall of Reality

1. Francis A. Schaeffer, *The God Who Is There* (Downers Grove, IL: InterVarsity Press, 2020), 93.

2. Jaqueline Terrebonne, "How Avant-Garde Composer John Cage Reimagined Sound While Mushroom Foraging," *Galerie*, June 25, 2020, https://galerie magazine.com/john-cage-mushroom-foraging-book/.

3. Calvin Tompkins, from an unidentified article published in the *New Yorker*, November 28, 1964, as quoted in Schaeffer, *The God Who Is There*, 94.

4. Stephen Hicks, "The Postmodern Assault on Reason," Atlas Society, June 16, 2010, https://www.atlassociety.org/post/the-postmodern-assault-on-reason.
5. Hicks, "Postmodern Assault on Reason."
6. Denyse O'Leary, "Why Can't Winston Count?" *Salvo*, Winter 2020, https://salvomag.com/article/salvo55/why-cant-winston-count.
7. Kim Charlton (@LogicalPoetry), "Standards Aren't Objective," Twitter, July 7, 2020, 11:13 a.m., https://twitter.com/LogicalPoetry/status /1280535419801591808.
8. Hicks, "Postmodern Assault on Reason."
9. Richard Dawkins, *The Blind Watchmaker* (New York: W. W. Norton, 1986), 1.
10. Dawkins, *The Blind Watchmaker*, 21.
11. Richard Dawkins, *The Selfish Gene* (New York: Oxford University Press, 1989), 3.
12. Robert Wright, *The Moral Animal* (New York: Knopf Doubleday, 1995), 216.
13. Stephen Hawking and Leonard Mlodinow, *The Grand Design* (New York: Bantam Books, 2010), 32.
14. Stephen Hawking, *Black Holes and Baby Universes and Other Essays* (New York: Bantam Books, 1993), 134.
15. Hawking, *Black Holes and Baby Universes*, 132.
16. Quoted by James K. A. Smith in *How (Not) to Be Secular* (Grand Rapids, MI: Eerdmans, 2014), 85.
17. C. S. Lewis, *That Hideous Strength* (New York: Scribner, 1945, 1974), 355–356.
18. "Extract Eric Fromm on Conscience as Disobedience," Philosophical Investigations, July 21, 2009, 4, https://peped.org/philosophical investigations/extract-eric-fromm-on-conscience-as-disobedience/4.
19. "Extract Eric Fromm on Conscience as Disobedience."
20. "Nietzsche: The Conscience," Bartleby Research, accessed January 20, 2022, https://www.bartleby.com/essay/Nietzsche-the-Conscience -FKUS293RZZS.
21. Voltaire to Frederick William II, King of Prussia, November 28, 1770, in *Digital Correspondence of Voltaire*, eds. N. Cronk and R. V. McNamee, trans. S. G. Tallentyre (Electronic Enlightenment Project: 2014), http:// www.e-enlightenment.com/item/voltfrFE5010231a2c.
22. Joseph Conrad, *Under Western Eyes* (Peterborough, ON: Broadview, 2010), 74.
23. Robert Green Ingersoll, *The Works of Robert G. Ingersoll: Political* (New York: Dresden Publishing, 1902), 429.

24. Quoted in Saraswathy Nagarajan, "'We Are Not Leaving the Scene':
    Parvathy," The Hindu, November 1, 2018, https://www.thehindu.com
    /entertainment/movies/actor-parvathy-says-she-wont-cow-down-to
    -bullying/article25390490.ece.
25. William Shakespeare, *Hamlet*, act 1, scene 3, lines 79–80.
26. Richard Selzer, "What I Saw at the Abortion," *Esquire*, January 1976, 67.
27. Wright, *Moral Animal*, 216.

Chapter 4: The Elephant in the Room

1. This story appears in several unverified accounts. Its earliest attribution
   to William James seems to be in Don E. Gibbons and John F. Connelly,
   Selected Readings in Psychology (St. Louis, MO: Mosby Publishing, 1970),
   ch. 11. Several websites question the authenticity of the story, some
   attributing it to persons other than William James.
2. C. S. Lewis, *Miracles: A Preliminary Study* (New York: Macmillan, 1947), 27.
   Italics are in the original.
3. Neil Postman, *Amusing Ourselves to Death: Public Discourse in the Age of
   Show Business* (New York: Penguin, 1985).

Chapter 5: The Mystifying Mystery of Morality

1. Bill Gates, interview by David Frost, Celebrity Atheist List, November 1995,
   http://www.celebatheists.com/wiki/Bill_Gates.
2. Fyodor Dostoyevsky, *The Brothers Karamazov*, trans. Andrew R. McAndrew
   (New York: Bantam Books, 1970), 95.
3. William Lane Craig, "The Indispensability of Meta-Ethical Foundations
   for Morality," *Foundations* 5 (1997): 9–12.
4. V. I. Lenin, quoted by Kevin D. Williamson, "The Kulaks Must Be
   Liquidated as a Class," *National Review*, January 25, 2019, https://www
   .nationalreview.com/2019/01/elizabeth-warren-tax-plan-is-asset-forfeiture/.
5. Richard Taylor, *Ethics, Faith, and Reason* (Englewood Cliffs: Prentice-Hall,
   1985), 2–3.

Chapter 6: The Mind-Bending Mystery of Origins

1. Ivan Couronne and Issam Ahmed, "Top Cosmologist's Lonely Battle against
   'Big Bang' Theory," Phys.org, November 14, 2019, https://phys.org/news
   /2019-11-cosmologist-lonely-big-theory.html.
2. "Big Bang Theory," All about Science, accessed December 20, 2019,
   https://www.big-bang-theory.com.
3. Stephen Hawking and Leonard Mlodinow, *The Grand Design* (New York:
   Bantam Books, 2010), 180.

4. Natalie Wolchover, "Physicists Debate Hawking's Idea That the Universe Had No Beginning," Quanta Magazine, June 6, 2019, https://www.quantamagazine.org/physicists-debate-hawkings-idea-that-the-universe-had-no-beginning-20190606/.

5. Dorian Sagan, "Life," Encyclopedia Britannica, January 27, 2022, https://www.britannica.com/science/life.

6. "Abiogenesis," Biology Online, February 27, 2021, https://www.biologyonline.com/dictionary/abiogenesis.

7. John Horgan, "Pssst! Don't Tell the Creationists, but Scientists Don't Have a Clue How Life Began," Cross-Check (blog), Scientific American, February 28, 2011, https://blogs.scientificamerican.com/cross-check/pssst-dont-tell-the-creationists-but-scientists-dont-have-a-clue-how-life-began/.

8. Nola Taylor Tillman, "Origin of Life Probed in Scientific Contest," Space.com, June 26, 2012, https://www.space.com/16311-origins-of-life-challenge-winners.html.

9. George M. Whitesides, "Revolutions in Chemistry: Priestley Medalist George M. Whitesides' Address," Chemical and Engineering News 85 (March 26, 2007): 12–17, quoted by Casey Luskin in "Top Five Problems with Current Origin-of-Life Theories," Evolution News & Science Today, December 12, 2012, https://evolutionnews.org/2012/12/top_five_probl/.

10. Kara Rogers, "Abiogenesis," Encyclopedia Britannica, updated September 26, 2018, https://www.britannica.com/science/abiogenesis.

11. Committee on the Limits of Organic Life in Planetary Systems, Committee on the Origins and Evolution of Life, National Research Council, The Limits of Organic Life in Planetary Systems (Washington, DC: National Academy Press, 2007), 60, quoted by Casey Luskin, "Top Five Problems with Current Origin-of-Life Theories," Evolution News & Science Today, December 12, 2012, https://evolutionnews.org/2012/12/top_five_probl/.

12. Casey Luskin, "Top Five Problems with Current Origin-of-Life Theories," Evolution News & Science Today, December 12, 2012, https://evolutionnews.org/2012/12/top_five_probl/.

13. Luskin, "Top Five Problems with Current Origin-of-Life Theories."

14. Harold Urey, Christian Science Monitor, January 4, 1962, quoted in Moshe Averick, "Speculation, Faith, and Unproven Assumptions: The History of Origin of Life Research in Scientists' Own Words," The Algemeiner, September 27, 2012, https://www.algemeiner.com/2012/09/27/speculation-faith-and-unproven-assumptions-the-history-of-origin-of-life-research-in-scientists-own-words/.

15. G. K. Chesterton, Delphi Complete Works of G. K. Chesterton (Hastings, East Sussex: Delphi Classics, 2013).

16. Hawking and Mlodinow, *The Grand Design*, 135.
17. W. Wayt Gibbs, "Profile: George F. R. Ellis," *Scientific American* 273, no. 4 (October 1995): 55.
18. C. S. Lewis, "The Laws of Nature," *God in the Dock* (Grand Rapids, MI: Eerdmans, 1970), 77.

Chapter 7: The Hotel That Charlie Built

1. Thomas Hayden et al., "A Theory Evolves: How Evolution Really Works, and Why It Matters More Than Ever," *U.S. News and World Report*, July 29, 2002, 43.
2. Phillip E. Johnson, *Objections Sustained* (Downers Grove, IL: InterVarsity Press, 1998), 20.
3. George G. Simpson, "The Nonprevalence of Humanoids," *Science* 143 (1964): 770.
4. "The Origin of Birds," *Understanding Evolution*, accessed December 12, 2019, https://evolution.berkeley.edu/evolibrary/article/evograms_06.
5. Colin Patterson, quoted in Christopher H. K. Persaud, *Evolution: Beyond the Realm of Real Science* (Maitland, FL: Xulon, 2007), 86.
6. Charles Darwin, *The Origin of Species* (New York: Oxford University Press, 1998), 141.
7. Robert H. Rastall, "Geology," *Encyclopedia Britannica*, vol. 10 (1949), 168, quoted by John C. Whitcomb and Henry M. Morris, *The Genesis Flood* (Phillipsburg, NJ: P & R Publishing, 2010), 134.
8. Richard Dawkins, *The Blind Watchmaker* (New York: Norton, 1986), 229.
9. Mark Ridley, "Who Doubts Evolution," *New Scientist* 90, no. 1259 (June 25, 1981): 831.
10. Pierre-Paul Grassé, *Evolution of Living Organisms* (New York: Academic Press, 1977), 31.
11. Colin Patterson, in a letter to Luther Sunderland, April 10, 1979, quoted in Luther D. Sunderland, *Darwin's Enigma: Fossils and Other Problems* (El Cajon, CA: Master Books, 1988), 89.
12. Richard Carrier, "How Did Male and Female Reproductive Systems Develop at the Same Time in Separate Organisms Accidentally? The Atheist Perspective," The God Contention, accessed December 6, 2019, https://www.godcontention.org/atheist/how-did-male-and-female -reproductive-systems-develop-at-the-same.
13. Emily C. Dooley, "Study Challenges Evolutionary Theory that DNA Mutations Are Random," ScienceDaily, University of California–Davis, January 12, 2022, https://www.sciencedaily.com/releases/2022/01 /220112121512.htm.

14. Graham Bell, *The Masterpiece of Nature: The Evolution of Genetics and Sexuality*, quoted in "Evolution of Sex—the Dilemma," All about Science, accessed December 6, 2021, https://www.allaboutscience.org/evolution-of-sex.htm.
15. "Evolution of Sex—the Dilemma."
16. "Introduction and Responses to Criticism of Irreducible Complexity," Discovery Institute, February 20, 2006, https://www.discovery.org/a/3408/.
17. Dooley, "Study Challenges Evolutionary Theory."
18. Stephen Meyer, quoted in Lee Strobel, *The Case for a Creator* (Grand Rapids, MI: Zondervan, 2004), 224.
19. Meyer, quoted in Strobel, *The Case for a Creator*, 237.
20. Meyer, quoted in Strobel, *The Case for a Creator*, 282.
21. Lee Spetner, quoted in "DNA Evidence for Evolution," All about Creation, accessed December 28, 2019, https://www.allaboutcreation.org/dna-evidence-for-evolution-faq.htm.
22. Michael Behe, *Darwin Devolves: The New Science about DNA That Challenges Evolution* (New York: HarperOne, 2019).
23. Meyer, quoted in Strobel, *The Case for a Creator*, 243.
24. Wolfgang Smith, *Teilhardism and the New Religion: A Thorough Analysis of the Teachings of Pierre Teilhard de Chardin* (Gastonia, NC: TAN Books, 2015), 18.
25. "A Scientific Dissent from Darwinism," A Scientific Dissent from Darwinism, accessed January 26, 2022, https://dissentfromdarwin.org.
26. "A Scientific Dissent."
27. Phillip E. Johnson, *Objections Sustained: Subversive Essays on Evolution, Law & Culture* (Downers Grove, IL: InterVarsity Press, 1998), 9, 25.
28. Dawkins, *Blind Watchmaker*, 6.
29. Doug Stewart, "Thirty-four Great Scientists Who Were Committed Christians," Famous Scientists, accessed December 26, 2019, https://www.famousscientists.org/great-scientists-christians/.
30. D. M. S. Watson, "Adaptation," *Nature*, August 10, 1929, 233.
31. George Wald, "The Origin of Life," *Scientific American*, August 1954, 44–53, quoted in "The Quote Mine Project," The Talk Origins Archive, accessed January 26, 2022, http://www.talkorigins.org/faqs/quotes/mine/part1-4.html#quote57.
32. Summarized from "The Quote Mine Project," The Talk Origins Archive, 2006, http://www.talkorigins.org/faqs/quotes/mine/part4-2.html.
33. David Catchpoole, "Dawkins and Design," Creation.com, June 6, 2009, https://creation.com/dawkins-and-design.

34. Thomas Nagel, *The Last Word* (New York: Oxford University Press, 1997), 130.
35. Richard Lewontin, "Billions and Billions of Demons," *New York Review of Books*, January 9, 1997, 28.
36. Aldous Huxley, "Confessions of a Professed Atheist," *Report: Perspective on the News,* vol. 3 (June 1966), 19.
37. Johnson, *Darwin on Trial*, 120–123.
38. Malcolm Muggeridge, "Pascal Lectures," delivered at University of Waterloo, Ontario, Canada, 1978.

Chapter 8: Reason's Exiled Ally

1. J. P. Moreland, *Love Your God with All Your Mind* (Colorado Springs, CO: NavPress, 1997), 25.
2. Phil Zuckerman, "Does It Take Faith to Be an Atheist?" *Psychology Today*, September 22, 2016, https://www.psychologytoday.com/us/blog/the -secular-life/201609/does-it-take-faith-be-atheist.
3. Becky Garrison, "What It Means to Be Moral: Why Religion Is Not Necessary for Living an Ethical Life," *The Humanist*, August 27, 2019, https://the humanist.com/magazine/september-october-2019/arts_entertainment/what -it-means-to-be-moral-why-religion-is-not-necessary-for-living-an-ethical-life/.
4. Phil Zuckerman, "What Does 'Secular' Mean?" *Psychology Today*, July 28, 2014, https://www.psychologytoday.com/us/blog/the-secular-life/201407 /what-does-secular-mean.
5. Thomas Nagel, *The Last Word* (New York: Oxford University Press, 1997), 130.
6. G. K. Chesterton, *The Autobiography of G. K. Chesterton* (San Francisco: Ignatius Press, 1936), 217.
7. Edwin A. Abbott, *Flatland* (New York: Dover Publications, 1952).
8. Loren Eiseley, *The Unexpected Universe* (New York: Harcourt Brace, 1964), 117.
9. Carl Sagan, *Cosmos: A Personal Voyage*, episode 1, "The Shores of the Cosmic Ocean," 1980, video, 3:15, https://ihavenotv.com/the-shores -of-the-cosmic-ocean-cosmos-a-personal-voyage.

Chapter 9: The Unquenchable Desire for Camelot

1. Dan Bova, "Stephen Hawking Says Humans Have 1,000 Years Left on Earth," *Entrepreneur*, November 18, 2016, https://www.entrepreneur.com /article/285432.
2. Adapted from Dr. David Jeremiah, "The Futility of Life," Sermons.love, accessed November 25, 2019, https://sermons.love/david-jeremiah/4431 -david-jeremiah-the-futility-of-life.html.

3. Carl Jung, *Modern Man in Search of a Soul* (Eastford, CT: Martino Fine, 2017), 70.
4. Michael M. Phillips, "Lysol Factory Job Becomes a Calling. 'Hey, I Work at the Place That Makes That,'" *Wall Street Journal*, April 21, 2020, https://www.wsj.com/articles/the-workers-at-a-lysol-plant-have-a-mission-now-11587482618.
5. Pope John Paul II, *Centesimus Annus*, May 1, 1991, quoted by J. Daryl Charles in "John Paul II at 100," *Touchstone* 33, no. 5 (September/October 2020): 35.
6. Rick Gore, "The Once and Future Universe," *National Geographic*, June 1983, 748.
7. John Updike, "The Future of Faith: Confessions of a Churchgoer," *New Yorker*, November 29, 1999, 88.
8. Aldous Huxley, "Confessions of a Professed Atheist," *Report: Perspective on the News*, vol. 3 (June 1966), 19.
9. Bkekakis, "Actors Who Committed Suicide," IMDB.com, January 29, 2017, https://www.imdb.com/list/ls062335622/; "George Sanders, Film Villain, a Suicide," *New York Times*, April 26, 1972, https://www.nytimes.com/1972/04/26/archives/george-sanders-film-villain-a-suicide.html.

Chapter 10: The Key to Reveling in Beauty and Joy
1. "Fallen Angels: Concorde, a Transport Icon," The Beauty of Transport, February 17, 2016, https://thebeautyoftransport.com/2016/02/17/fallen-angels-concorde-a-transport-icon/.
2. George John Romanes, *Thoughts on Religion* (Chicago: Open Court, 1895), 29.
3. "A Story about Coleridge," *Jamesian Philosophy Refreshed*, December 27, 2013, http://jamesian58.blogspot.com/2013/12/a-story-about-coleridge.html.
4. C. S. Lewis, *The Abolition of Man* (New York: HarperCollins, 1944, 1974), 5.
5. In this section you may detect echoes of C. S. Lewis's unparalleled masterpiece "The Weight of Glory" (in C. S. Lewis, *The Weight of Glory*, New York: HarperOne, 2001). If so, your senses do not deceive you. We gratefully acknowledge our debt to this essay for the central thoughts developed in this section.
6. "The Lost Chord," Gilbert and Sullivan Archive, accessed February 7, 2022, https://www.gsarchive.net/sullivan/songs/lost_chord/chord.html.
7. Robert Frost, "Stopping by Woods on a Snowy Evening," Poetry Foundation, accessed February 7, 2022, https://www.poetryfoundation.org/poems/42891/stopping-by-woods-on-a-snowy-evening.

est descriptions of the prophecies and evidences surrounding Christ's birth, death, and Resurrection, see Josh McDowell and Sean McDowell, *Evidence That Demands a Verdict* (Nashville, TN: Thomas Nelson, 2017).

276

ABOUT THE AUTHORS

As a young man, **JOSH D. McDOWELL** considered himself an agnostic.

He truly believed that Christianity was worthless. However, when challenged to intellectually examine the claims of Christianity, Josh discovered compelling, overwhelming evidence for the reliability of the Christian faith. After trusting in Jesus Christ as Savior and Lord, Josh's life changed dramatically as he experienced the power of God's love.

After Josh's conversion, his plans for law school turned instead to plans to tell a doubting world about the truth of Jesus Christ. After studying at Kellogg College, Josh completed his college degree at Wheaton College and then attended Talbot Theological Seminary (now Talbot School of Theology), where he graduated magna cum laude with a master of divinity degree.

In 1961, Josh joined the staff of Campus Crusade for Christ International. Not long after, he started the Josh

McDowell Ministry to reach young people worldwide with the truth and love of Jesus.

Well known as an articulate speaker, Josh has addressed more than 46 million people, giving over 27,200 talks in 139 countries.

As he traveled to other countries, Josh quickly realized that where people were sick, homeless, and hungry, words were not enough. In 1991, Josh founded Operation Carelift to meet the physical and spiritual needs he discovered in orphanages, hospitals, schools, and prisons in the countries of the former Soviet Union. Since that time, Operation Carelift has delivered humanitarian aid (food, clothing, and medical supplies) worth more than $46 million. Nearly one million children have received school supplies, food items, hygiene items, and toys from the volunteers that travel twice a year to share God's love with them.

Josh has received two significant honors from the Russian people because of these efforts. He is the only non-Russian to receive an honorary doctor of pediatrics degree from the Russian Academy of Medicine—in recognition of his work among the children of Russia. Also, Josh is the only foreigner to become a member of the prestigious Russian Club of Scientists. Operation Carelift, which has grown into one of the largest humanitarian aid organizations based in the United States, is now a part of UNTO (formerly known as Global Aid Network).

In the United States, Josh and his team have created many cutting-edge live events to help young people stand strong and firm in their faith in the face of a rapidly changing culture. These have often developed into full-blown campaigns, such as:

Six Hours with Josh
Why Wait?
Counter the Culture
Right from Wrong
Beyond Belief

Since 1960, Josh has written or coauthored 151 books in 128 languages, including:

More Than a Carpenter—over 27 million copies distributed
Evidence That Demands a Verdict—named one of the twentieth century's top 40 books and one of the 13 most influential books of the last 50 years on Christian thought by *World* magazine

In addition to many other awards, Josh has been nominated 36 times for the Gold Medallion Christian Book of the Year and has received that award on 4 occasions.

In spite of all the honors and awards he has received, Josh will tell anyone that his greatest joys and pleasures come from his family. He and his wife, Dottie, have been married 48 years. They have 4 children and 10 grandchildren.

Josh McDowell Ministry is a Cru ministry (the US division of Campus Crusade for Christ International).

THOMAS WILLIAMS has enjoyed two thriving careers, first as an artist and second as an author and editor. In both careers he specialized in work for Christian publishers. As an artist, he designed or illustrated more than 1,500 book covers and jackets. He served as art director for two Christian publishers and won CBA's best book cover award six times. His portrait of C. S. Lewis hangs in the Wade Center at Wheaton College.

As an author, Tom has written fifteen books, fiction and nonfiction, published by Word, Zondervan, Thomas Nelson, Tyndale, Baker/Revell, and Lillenas. Four of these were cowritten with Josh McDowell and one with Michael W. Smith. One of his own was a national bestseller, staying on the ECPA list five months and reaching the number two position. In addition to his own books, Tom has edited or collaborated on dozens of books by several Christian authors. He has also written articles for denominational publications and *Touchstone* magazine. He has been interviewed on several radio stations, appeared on Daystar's *Joni Table Talk*, and delivered lectures at two universities.

Always an avid reader, Tom was early influenced by the writings of C. S. Lewis, G. K. Chesterton, and George MacDonald. Throughout his adult life, he has been active in his church, serving as a deacon or an elder and often teaching classes.

Tom and his late wife, Faye, raised three daughters. Now semiretired, he still writes, edits, paints, and teaches. He enjoys hanging out with his daughters, sons-in-law, and eight grandchildren; listening to good music; reading; watching old movies; and traveling. He lives in Dallas, Texas.

Share the Story.

With over 15 million copies in print, this modern classic

has introduced countless people to Jesus. Now, in this newly

updated version, Josh McDowell is joined by his son, Sean,

as they reexamine the evidence for today's generation:

Is Jesus really the Lord he claimed to be?

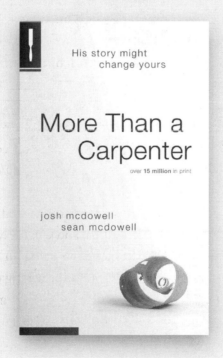

Serving others until the whole world hears about Jesus.

Josh McDowell
A CRU MINISTRY